AMERICAN PROFILES

MILITARY LEADERS SINCE WORLD WAR II

C. W. Borklund

Facts On File
New York • Oxford

Military Leaders Since World War II

Copyright © 1992 by C. W. Borklund

All rights reserved. No part of this book may be reproduced or utilized in any form or by any means, electronic or mechanical, including photocopying, recording, or by any information storage or retrieval systems, without permission in writing from the publisher. For information contact:

Facts On File, Inc.
460 Park Avenue South
New York NY 10016
USA

Facts On File Limited
c/o Roundhouse Publishing Ltd.
P.O. Box 140
Oxford OX2 7SF
United Kingdom

Library of Congress Cataloging-in-Publication Data
Borklund, Carl W.
   Military leaders since World War II / by C.W. Borklund
      p. cm. — (American profiles)
   Includes bibliographical references and index.
   Summary: Describes the careers of eleven modern American military figures, including Colin Powell, William Westmoreland, Edward Rowny, and James Abrahamson.
   ISBN 0-8160-2606-8
   1. Generals—United States—Biography—Juvenile literature.
   2. Admirals—United States—Biography—Juvenile literature.
   3. United States—Armed Forces—Biography—Juvenile literature.
   [1. United States—Armed Forces—Biography. 2. Generals.
   3. Admirals.] I. Title. II. Series: American profiles (Facts On File, Inc.
E840.4.B67 1992
355'.0092'2—dc20
[B]   91-41403

A British CIP catalogue record for this book is available from the British Library.

Facts On File books are available at special discounts when purchased in bulk quantities for businesses, associations, institutions or sales promotions. Please contact our Special Sales Department in New York at 212/683-2244 (dial 800/322-8755 except in NY, AK or HI) or in Oxford at 865/728399.

Text design by Ron Monteleone
Jacket design by Ron Monteleone
Composition by Facts On File, Inc./Grace Ferrara
Manufactured by the Maple-Vail Book Manufacturing Group
Printed in the United States of America

10 9 8 7 6 5 4 3 2 1

This book is printed on acid-free paper.

Contents

Acknowledgments v

Introduction vii

General Colin L. Powell 1

General Matthew B. Ridgway 11

General William C. Westmoreland 22

General Creighton W. Abrams 34

General Edward L. Rowny 45

Admiral Arleigh A. Burke 56

Admiral Thomas H. Moorer 67

Vice Admiral John T. Hayward 78

General Lewis W. Walt 90

General George S. Brown 101

Lieutenant General James A. Abrahamson 113

Index 125

To
Carl E. Borklund
1904–1954

*"His name ain't on no tablets;
In no park his statue stands.
All his life he grubbed for wages;
You could tell it by his hands.
And the things he left behind him
Wouldn't fill a sardine can.
But I'd like to got to thank him
Just for bein' my old man."*
—*Anonymous*

Acknowledgments

The author of this book received a great deal of voluntary, invaluable help compiling it. The still-living military leaders' recollections and guidance were a key, of course. So was the information and opinion given freely, over several hours of their time, by dozens of others—friends, former commanders of, or subordinates to, the leaders profiled here. (Many of those deserve the distinction of "military leader.")

Dr. Alfred Goldberg, the Pentagon's chief historian, helped steer me along a quick, efficient path to Facts On File, so to speak, in the Pentagon, Army, Navy, Marine Corps, and Air Force History libraries. Obviously, sifting through their masses of data was essential to completing this book.

Gathering up the pictures for this book was possibly the most fun, like thumbing through somebody else's old family album. Bettie Sprigg, in the Office of the Assistant Secretary of Defense for Public Affairs, made it that way, partly because she's a wizard at knowing where all those old albums are filed. Beyond her aid, the National Archives and the military history libraries' photo sections were helpful, particularly those staffers who "worked the problem" in the photo lab of Dr. Dean Allard's Naval Historical Center.

A special recognition should go to the wives, not only of those leaders highlighted here, but military wives generally. The nomadic life; the days, months, even years apart; the assaults by enemies abroad or mostly political opponents at home; all put terrible strains on a marriage. Many don't survive, so most of those that do are special. Maybe a book should be written about military wives—there's material enough. Two of the several gathered, researching for this book, come quickly to mind.

One is Mary Rita Leyko, wife of Ambassador/General Edward Rowny. She suffered a crippling stroke in 1979, the year Rowny resigned in protest against the proposed SALT II arms treaty. They worked together, hard, on her recovery; and "cried tears of joy," says Rowny, some weeks later, when she was able to say "apple" plainly. She died of cancer in 1988. Several people, I discovered, shared one general's opinion that "Rita Rowny was bright, full of energy, a terrific judge of people. She would have been a success in any career she chose; she chose to be Ed Rowny's wife and the mother of their five children."

Joint Chiefs Chairman George Brown said pretty much the same about his wife, Alice "Skip" Calhoun, in a letter to some 1,000 people at an Air Force Association banquet. Summoned to duty, he had sent "Skip" to receive for him its highest honor, the H. H. Arnold Award. Said Brown's letter, in part:

> *What I have accomplished over these years has been with her faith, trust, and full support. In a sense, she represents all of the fine wives who fulfill their roles so graciously and competently that their men are free to go around, receiving awards such as this one . . .*
> —*C. W. Borklund*

Introduction

The Pentagon (Department of Defense photo by MSGT Ken Hammond USAF)

American history has been a fertile field for displays of military skill and leadership. Yet, from roughly 1775 through the end of World War II in 1945, "military leaders" in the United States have been identified mostly as the people who planned battles, then led combat forces in them to victory. And winning a war always meant two things afterwards: most of the war machine would be trashed; most of the people sent home. However, this uniquely American practice was not repeated, at least not so completely, after World War II. Toward the end of that most destructive war in history, military leaders such as Army General George C. Marshall and Secretary of the Navy James V. Forrestal had begun to warn the country that, this time, victory would not bring the same kind of peace it had before.[1]

---

[1]After the war, Marshall served as secretary of state for a time and was also awarded a Nobel Peace Prize; Forrestal, in 1947, became the first secretary of defense.

Military Leaders Since World War II

Instead, they and other government leaders predicted the new "peace" would see a World War II ally, the Soviet Union, turn into an avowed enemy. Further, they forecast, it would attempt to expand its military power and increase its political influence beyond the so-called Communist bloc of countries it already controlled in Eastern Europe. Its first targets, they argued, would be countries on its borders already impoverished by the war, i.e., in Western Europe, the Middle East, and Asia.

By 1947, that forecast had begun to come true. A group of mostly Western powers—rearmed, bound together by mutual-defense treaties, and led by the United States—was assembled to derail Soviet expansionism. Nobody wanted the military part of this confrontation to degenerate into a nuclear World War III. But, none of them wanted their countries taken over by Communist rulers at the point of a gun either.

A new phrase, "The Cold War," was coined to describe this constantly shifting, ever-boiling conflict. It has had profound implications for the American military and its leaders. Out of the Cold War sprang, for one thing, a modern defense organization. Along with it has come a greater appreciation for the complexities of preserving national security.

A succinct summary of the pressures the Cold War has imposed on today's military leader can be found in a two-paragraph section of the *First Report* [to Congress] *of the Secretary of Defense*, published in 1948. In it, Forrestal wrote:

> *National Security cannot be measured today in terms of the United States alone. It must be measured in terms of the whole world. The prerequisite of world peace is world stability. An unstable world endangers our security because we are no longer isolated—if we ever were—in an age of aircraft of supersonic speed and of the indicated developments in the field of guided missiles and of submarines of transoceanic range. The advances of science have wiped out the old barriers of time and space, oceans and icecaps.*
>
> *It is not enough for us merely to devise what we hope will be an impregnable defense against new weapons and methods of warfare. As a primary precaution against war, we must strive to prevent its inception anywhere. We must do everything we can to bring order out of chaos wherever it exists and to eradicate the evils and injustices which cause war.*

In effect, all these trends have expanded the range of skills military leaders require to be effective in today's world. They need

Introduction

to be well versed in national and international politics. They need the ability to direct efficiently a research, development, and manufacturing enterprise larger than any private commercial company. They need some knowledge of budgeting and accounting. They need to know the strengths and weaknesses of both the U.S. industrial base and that of would-be allies and adversaries overseas. (As Forrestal once noted, "National security can no more be divorced from economics than it can from diplomacy.")

Possibly most important of all, they must be skilled at one of the toughest games there is: the selling of new ideas; of the need for a new weapon system or force structure to handle the ever changing threats to national security. A military leader must be eloquent and convincing to civilian superiors in the Pentagon, in the White House, and in the Congress, for these are the people who decide what United States military forces should be able to do.

The military leaders chosen for this book were adroit at getting their tough-minded, usually expensive, plans for national security planted high on the budgetary priority list. Or, at the very least, they got their schemes entered into the public debate.

The Cold War did not erase one historical test of military leadership, however. It fact, the need for that age-old talent, leadership in combat, became more important than ever before. "Morale! Elan! *Esprit de Corps!*," Marshall thundered once, "With it, anything is possible. Without it, nothing is possible." In short, to prevent war, a military leader in the United States still had to convince both his own people and a potential enemy that, if forced to, he could fight and win battles.

Most of the officers chosen for this book have earned a chestful of medals, awarded for careers of outstanding service in difficult and often deadly work. President George Washington said, in 1790, "To be prepared for war is one of the most effective means of preserving peace." Having a reputation as a winner can be stronger insurance against war than a warehouse full of weapons.

That talent is not widely recognized, however, for several reasons. One of those is current law, which says, basically, that the principal task of senior military leaders today is not to command troops, but to be advisers to higher, civilian authorities. "Staff work" rarely attracts public notice.

Moreover, the U.S. military's main mission today, helping prevent war, doesn't earn military advisers praise very often either. It would be somewhat like the coach thanking his team for protesting the coin toss at a high school football game. Thus, in 1983, when asked what the Pentagon's biggest problem was, then–Deputy Secretary of Defense Paul Thayer answered, "Our biggest problem is we're not making any heroes, anymore."

None of this is to say there hasn't been a wealth of good military leaders since World War II. Those profiled in this book are particularly remarkable examples; but at least a dozen or so more would fit this book's title just as well. Moreover, the historical record argues most U.S. military leaders always have needed some, if not all, of these nominally "non-military" talents.

What is new today is the explosive growth in scientific and engineering know-how since World War II. In short, with technology having jumped the once-protective moats of the oceans, the old military instruction to "Go with what you already have" has taken on new, ominous meaning. On the other hand, as today's military leaders know very well, merely tapping the rush of technology does not translate overnight into more powerfully effective military forces. It's more like buying a car, but not being allowed to drive it until "Dad," the Congress, makes the final payment.

For instance, the Army's Patriot anti-missile missile performed impressively in 1991 against the Iraqi Scud missile in the Persian Gulf War. But, in fact, the Patriot is merely a slight product improvement of the Army's Sergeant and Sprint anti-ballistic missiles developed in the late 1960s. Similar histories could be written about virtually every other major strategic and tactical weapons system in the U.S. military inventory—not to mention a long list of those which still languish in the laboratory, old paper promises to the troops which have never come true. As Admiral Arleigh Burke has summarized sharply, "The budget is everything. Without a budget, you don't have anything."

Further, creation of the Army/Air Force "Airland" battle doctrine, used so effectively in the Persian Gulf War, was first ordered into being by Generals Creighton Abrams and George Brown in 1973 when they were Chiefs of Staff of, respectively, the Army and the Air Force. A similar record is in Pentagon files, covering proposals to develop a military capability to transport "a clearly overwhelming military force" quickly halfway around the world—as was done in the Persian Gulf in 1990–91. The proposal was approved "in concept" 30 years ago by the

Introduction

Pentagon's civilian leadership, the White House, and Congress. It has been routinely underfunded every year since.

An almost routine risk of military leaders since World War II is their struggle to get their innovations on—and kept on—the Pentagon's and Congress' shopping lists. People who propose new ideas attract criticism, often very personal criticism, in every walk of life. In the military, there also is the high probability that, long before a new plan, or weapons system has been accepted, the military leader who promoted it will be only a memory in a Pentagon filing cabinet.

As former Secretary of Defense Thomas S. Gates, Jr. noted in 1965, "Only history will tell how well any one of us did in one of these [top Pentagon] jobs, because we deal in futures. And [when the civilian and military leadership decides what to do] who knows, we may be right?" Basically, this book's intent is to document a little of that history.

Readers will find quotations throughout this book. To avoid cluttering the book with footnotes, none of those quotations are referenced as they occur. It may aid the reader doing further research to know that about 40 percent of those quoted remarks can be found in the bibliographical references at the end of each chapter. All the rest are first-person statements to the author by the person quoted.

What the Medals Mean

During their careers, the military leaders profiled in this book earned a small basketful of medals, as many as 35 or 40 in a few cases. Those include awards from some branch or other of the U.S. government for individual performance; "unit citations" for the deeds of the military unit to which the person was assigned and/or commanded at the time; and some presented to the individual by foreign governments.

Military Leaders Since World War II

To avoid what otherwise would seem endless repetition, only the U.S. military medals that carry the highest prestige are noted in this book's biographies. Further, the medal's initials, as shown below, will be used most of the time—as the Defense Department, itself, summarizes medals in its personnel files.

In addition, again for brevity's sake, when an individual was awarded more than one of some particular medal, a number will precede the initials. For example, the receipt of two Distinguished Service Medals will be cited simply as 2DSM rather than the more precise, "One Oak Leaf Cluster in lieu of a second Distinguished Service Medal."

The following are the most highly regarded U.S. military medals:

- *Medal of Honor*—awarded by the president at the instruction of Congress for an individual's "conspicuous gallantry and intrepidity at the risk of life and beyond the call of duty in actual conflict with the enemy."
- *Distinguished Service Cross* (DSC)—"for heroism and valor, involving extraordinary risk of life in connection with military operations against an enemy." (In the Navy, it also is known as the Navy Cross; and, in the Air Force as the Air Force Cross.)
- *Distinguished Service Medal* (DSM)—"for exceptionally meritorious service in a duty of great responsibility."
- *Silver Star* (SS)—"for distinguished gallantry in action."
- *Department of Defense Service Medal* (DDSM)—"for exceptionally meritorious service in a position of unique and great responsibility while serving on a joint staff or with other joint activities of the Department of Defense."
- *Defense Superior Service Medal* (DSSM)—"for superior, meritorious service on a joint staff or with other joint activities of the Department of Defense."
- *Legion of Merit* (LM)—"for exceptionally meritorious conduct in the performance of outstanding services."
- *Distinguished Flying Cross* (DFC)—"for distinguished heroism or extraordinary achievement while participating in aerial flight."
- *Soldier's Medal* as it's titled in the Army. (Called the *Navy Medal* and the *Marine Corps Medal* in those two services, respectively, it's known as the *Airman's Medal* in the Air Force.)—"for distinguished heroism not involving conflict with an enemy." (Once known as the Congressional *Silver Life-Saving Medal*, it is awarded, usually, for dramatic rescue of wounded and/or marooned persons "from a hostile environment.")

xii

Introduction

- *Bronze Star Medal* (BSM)—"for distinguished heroism or meritorious achievement in operations against an enemy or in support of such operations."
- *Purple Heart* (PH)—awarded to persons wounded in action against an enemy; or, subsequent to a Presidential decree made retroactive to December 6, 1941, awarded posthumously to those killed in action. (In and following World War I, the PH also was awarded to some persons who received a "meritorious service" certificate from the Commander-in-Chief, American Expeditionary Forces, in addition to those wounded in action. The PH also was awarded "for meritorious service other than wounds" at the outset of World War II—until September, 1942. Since then, by Presidential decree, the *Purple Heart* is awarded exclusively to persons killed or wounded in action against an enemy.)
- *Defense Meritorious Service Medal* (DMSM)—"for conspicuously meritorious service on joint staffs or other joint activities of the Department of Defense" (considered third in order of recognition behind the DDSM and the DSSM, respectively).
- *Meritorious Service Medal* (MSM)—"for conspicuously meritorious performance of duty in a non-combat situation."
- *Commendation Ribbon* (CR)—"for distinguished or meritorious service or meritorious achievement." (In the Army and Air Force, on March 31, 1960, they renamed this "Ribbon" to be their Commendation *Medal*.)

In addition to the above, awards also are presented to persons who demonstrate skill, leadership or heroism in a particular, specialized military field. Among the most prestigious of these:

- *Joint Service Commendation Medal* (JSCM)—"for outstanding performance of duty and meritorious achievement" by persons in uniform "while assigned to joint staffs" and/or "other joint activities."
- *Air Medal* (AM)—"for meritorious achievement beyond that normally expected, while participating in aerial flight." (The *Air Medal* can be earned by airborne infantry as well as aircraft pilots and flight crews.)
- *Combat Infantry Badge* (CIB)—"for exemplary conduct in combat against an enemy." In general, receipt of the award is restricted to infantrymen assigned or attached to an infan-

try combat unit of brigade size (approximately 3,500 persons) or smaller.
- *Combat Medical Badge* (CMB)—"for exemplary conduct" by Medical Corps personnel, i.e., doctors, nurses, and paramedics, while in support of an infantry unit (brigade size or smaller) during combat with enemy forces.

General Colin L. Powell

Colin Powell: "There are no secrets to success."
(Official Department of Defense photo by
R. D. Ward)

When Army General Colin Luther Powell was named Chairman of the Joint Chiefs of Staff on October 1, 1989, some editorial writers promptly labeled him the first black just-about-everything in American military history. The description was a bit overblown. Powell is, in fact, the first African-American to be military assistant to both the deputy secretary and the secretary of defense; the first to be White House assistant to the president for national security affairs; and the first to become Joint Chiefs chairman.[1]

---

[1] He is not the first African-American general in the modern-day military, however. President Franklin D. Roosevelt appointed Benjamin O. Davis to Army brigadier general in 1940. Davis' son, Davis, Jr., retired as an Air Force lieutenant general. And, in 1975, Daniel "Chappie" James, Jr., of the Air Force became the first African-American to reach four-star rank.

Much more impressive to most people in the Defense Department was another fact: Powell, they noted, had made brigadier general at age 42; and now, only 10 years later, was the youngest-ever four-star general to be designated the nation's top soldier.

"He is a remarkable man," said former President Ronald Reagan. "In wartime situations, he would be a great leader." Added then-U.S. Attorney General Edwin Meese, when Powell joined the White House staff in January 1987, "We'd have hired him whether he was black, white, or you-name-it. His perception of the needs for national security is simply superb."

For his part, Powell says, within the military family (he always emphasizes that distinction), "I have never felt there were people trying to hinder my progress" because of his racial origin. "I've been given the opportunity to compete fair and square. If some don't like the result, that's not my problem. That's their problem." It's a bit ironic that, 32 years earlier, Powell was not at all sure he wanted a career in the Army.

His parents, Luther Theophilus and Maud Ariel Powell, had imigrated from Jamaica to New York City in the 1920s. Powell was born there, in Harlem, on April 5, 1937. Shortly after he reached school age, the family moved to the South Bronx, "a step up in those days," he says. His father, a shipping clerk, and his mother, a seamstress, toiled six and seven days a week to give their children opportunities they never had. And the most important of those, they insisted, was a good education.

Still, Powell "horsed around a lot" in elementary and high school, he told newspaper columnist Carl Rowan; and his mediocre grades showed it. He went to college for only one reason: "My parents expected it; and, in my family, you did what they expected." And he had only one reason for entering the City College of New York rather than the more prestigious New York University: "NYU cost $750 a year then, and CCNY cost $20."

He graduated from City College in 1958 with a bachelor of science degree; but his course grades there were as dismal as those he had received from the New York public school system except for one, the college Reserve Officers Training Corps. "At CCNY I was attracted to ROTC and to a serious group within it, the Pershing Rifles. I found a home with them." He certainly did. He graduated at the top of his class in ROTC. "People tend to like to do," he chuckles today, "what they're good at doing."

General Colin L. Powell

Powell accepted an infantry second lieutenant's commission in June 1958, still thinking it was "just a job, a route out and up for me." And, in that context, he liked the Army's offer of rewards for doing what he enjoyed doing. Why the Army in particular? "I had seen seven years of war—World War II and Korea. That had made an indelible impression on me."

His first assignment was four months at Ft. Benning, Georgia, completing the infantry officers' basic training, the airborne, and the ranger courses. Even at that early stage, the results of his commitment began to show. He was awarded honors in the ranger course, for instance, a grueling test. (A team of 30 soldiers is airlifted into a hostile countryside where, for eight weeks, they have to think for themselves, fight simulated combat, and live off the land.)

During his four months in Georgia, Powell was shocked by, and suffered from, his first experiences in the harsh, demeaning realities of Southern racism. Segregation had been a textbook abstraction in the South Bronx where everybody—blacks, Hispanics, Jews—was a "minority." Cultural differences existed, of course, but neighbors were neighbors—mixing rather easily, even staying overnight at each other's homes. Powell even learned some Yiddish as a result. "I was stationed at Ft. Benning," he wrote later, "before I ever saw what is referred to as a 'White Anglo-Saxon Protestant.'"

From Ft. Benning, Powell was sent to Germany for two years; promoted to first lieutenant; then shipped to Ft. Devens in Massachusetts for two more years. In both places, he was given a combination of small-unit command and executive staff-officer jobs. This switching back and forth between "line" and "staff" assignments was, and still is, a career path designed to give aspiring young officers broad, yet detailed, knowledge of how all the parts in the Army machine are supposed to work together.

His last year at Ft. Devens, Powell became the battalion adjutant, usually a captain's job, because his commander found him "wise beyond his years in dealing with problems of morale and discipline." In 1962 he was promoted to captain. That was also the year he was transferred to the Army Special Warfare course at Ft. Bragg, North Carolina, and married Alma Vivian Johnson, whom he had met two years earlier on a blind date.

Next, he spent a year assigned to the U.S. Military Assistance Advisory Group, Vietnam as an adviser to a South Vietnamese infantry battalion. The U.S. military in Vietnam did not start sending its own forces into direct combat with the Communist North Vietnamese until after Congress passed the Gulf of Tonkin Resolution in late 1964. While Powell was there he was, technically, a noncombatant, teaching the South Vietnamese infantry how to fight. In truth, wrote French journalist Bernard Fall from Vietnam in 1961, "They [the Americans] may be called advisers, but they are fighting and dying out here."

At the end of 1963, when Powell returned to Ft. Benning, he brought with him firsthand knowledge of the killing cost of poor military leadership in jungle guerrilla warfare. Promoted to major in 1966, he was transferred to the Army Command and General Staff College in Ft. Leavenworth, Kansas, in 1967. He graduated a year later, second in his class of 1,244.

Back in Vietnam by June 1968, he was a battalion executive officer until the Americal Division commander read in a newspaper about his achievements. According to Rowan, that commander shouted at his aide, "I've got the number two Leavenworth graduate in my division, and he's stuck in the boonies? I want him on my staff!" Powell quickly became Americal deputy chief of staff, G-3 (combat operations planning). He would hear "I want you" a lot during the next 20 years from many other national security leaders, both military and civilian.

During the 1960s, Powell also took on a very personal commitment. Wrote former Secretary of Defense Caspar Weinberger in 1990, "He is not blind to America's faults. He has suffered under them—fighting a war in Vietnam we never intended to win; with his wife and family living [back in the United States] in the miserable conditions" of racial prejudice. "None of that embittered him [but it] did convince him he should fight harder to correct those faults, which he consistently has done."

His most-used tactic in his battle against racial bigotry is simply counseling African-American teenagers. Frequently, he offers them the career formula he is convinced will work for them as it has for him. "I've always strongly believed," he insists, "there are no secrets to success. Success is the result of preparation, hard work, learning from failure. My mother and father taught me those values, values which

General Colin L. Powell

generate good luck and opportunities. Of course, getting qualified, as 'Chappie' put it, is a great part of that."[2]

Beginning in September 1969, Powell spent a decade moving back and forth and around the world—the kind of merry-go-round that puts fierce strains on a wife and children. He commanded troops in Korea and at Ft. Campbell, Kentucky. He earned a master's of business administration at George Washington University and completed a one-year advanced course at the National War College. He was selected as a White House Fellow in 1972–73 (one of seven selected from among more than 1,500 applicants), working in the Office of Management and Budget (OMB).

The administrator of the OMB that year was Caspar Weinberger; the deputy administrator—Powell's immediate supervisor—was Frank Carlucci. Powell's intelligence and knowledge clearly impressed them both. When Weinberger and Carlucci became secretary and deputy secretary of defense, respectively, in the early 1980s, first Carlucci and, two years later, Weinberger asked Powell to be their military assistant.

Possibly the best summary of Powell's stellar reputation among the Pentagon's top civilian executives came not from one of those two men but from Army Brigadier General Peter Dawkins. Deputy director of the Army's Pentagon-based strategy, plans and policy office in the early 1980s, Dawkins told a *Washington Post* reporter, "As is the reality in any big organization like [the Defense Department], Colin could and did speak for the Secretary in some areas. I would meet him in his office and I would feel I had just been to the schoolmaster. He displayed the kind of virtuoso mastery of the political complexities of the Pentagon that is rare."

Powell escaped the Pentagon briefly in July 1986, to command the Army's 72,000-person Fifth Corps in Frankfurt, West Germany. But six months later Powell heard "I want you" again. Carlucci had become President Ronald Reagan's national security adviser and head of the White House National Security Council staff. He wanted Powell to be his deputy. A year later,

---

[2] A reference to the late General "Chappie" James whose standard lecture to African-American teenagers, in his last years, was "Get yourself qualified. That way, you take away the one weapon the bigot can use effectively against you. Get yourself qualified."

when Carlucci was appointed secretary of defense, Powell was President Reagan's choice to succeed Carlucci in the White House.

Being a military adviser, even at those high levels, may not seem like much. In fact, such a person can have a strong, sometimes decisive, influence over who will or will not do what in the national security business. The major reason for this is that high-level military advisers act as "keepers of the door." As many as 40 to 50 executives within the department have direct access to the secretary of defense. The president faces a similar demand on his time.

Even if the secretary of defense or the president could get away with granting an audience only to those subordinates, each would be fortunate to see him once every three weeks. On the other hand, the military adviser sees his boss every day, often several times a day. Sums up Powell, "The NSA [National Security Adviser] screens all advice coming to the President and makes sure the best of all that advice gets to him . . . All this makes the NSA, I'd also add, a very knowledgeable person."

Powell had to tap that knowledge quickly when he became chairman of the Joint Chiefs of Staff. On October 3, 1989, as Powell was being sworn into office, a citizen's uprising to overthrow Panamanian dictator Manuel Noriega erupted—and promptly collapsed for lack of U.S. military support. At that point, Powell had been consulting with General Maxwell Thurman, commander of the U.S. Southern Command in Panama, on strategy, tactics, and the kind of overwhelming military force that might be needed to handle "the Noriega problem."

At the same time, in the White House, he had strongly endorsed a State Department plan to offer Noriega immunity from prosecution on drug-smuggling charges in return for Noriega removing himself as dictator of Panama. (Powell has never backed risking American military lives if there was any other credible way to solve a problem.) Noriega spurned the offer, and declared that a state of war existed between the United States and Panama. While he blustered, one of his security patrols killed a U.S. Marine.

One day later, Powell walked into an Oval Office meeting; and announced, simply, "This time Noriega has gone too far." Said one unidentified official at the meeting, "[Powell] was unlike any other chairman new in the job. He just automatically understood the issues that were raised, the political, military and 'media' issues."

General Colin L. Powell

"People tend to like to do what they're good at doing," says Powell.
(Official Department of Defense photo by R. D. Ward)

Shortly thereafter, on December 20, President George Bush ordered 26,000 American Army, Navy, Marine Corps, and Air Force personnel into action. Within a week, they had Noriega in jail in Florida and had restored a democratically elected government to Panama—the clear, unambiguous mission they were assigned at the outset.

One year later, Powell was prepared again. In late August 1990, President Bush committed U.S. military forces to ousting the Iraqi occupation army from Kuwait and authorized use of the "clearly overwhelming force" Powell had requested. ("You win that way," Powell often has said, "at a much lower loss of life.")

At a Pentagon press conference in early 1991, just before the ground-attack phase of the war was launched, he told reporters, "We're going to surround the Iraqi army and then we're going to kill it." Instantly challenged, "How can your plan possibly work?," he answered simply, "Trust me. Trust me."

According to the *Washington Post*, as Powell said that, Joseph Schwar, a retired army colonel stationed 20 miles from Powell in Vietnam in 1968–69, heard it on TV as he walked through Dulles International Airport. "When he said, 'Trust me,' I said, 'Damn right; I know I can trust you.' And as I looked around, people were nodding and saying, 'If he says it, I can believe it.' That impressed me."[3]

The wars in Panama and the Persian Gulf clearly have confirmed that Powell is a first-rate military leader. Only future history will record if his decisions on longer-term issues were wise or not. But already the soundness of one of those is confirmed. Some 35 years ago, his father suggested he think about a government job. A big benefit from one of those, his father advised, is, "You can retire on a good pension." When Powell retires, his annual pension will exceed $52,000.

Chronology

April 5, 1937	Colin Luther Powell born in New York City
1958	graduates from City College of New York with a bachelor of science degree and an Army second lieutenant's commission
1962	promoted to captain after receiving specialized infantry training in the United States and Europe
1966	promoted to major after training and command assignments in Vietnam and at Ft. Benning, Georgia
1971	earns masters degree at George Washington University after promotion to lieutenant colonel

---

[3]Powell impressed the whole nation, apparently. Opinion polls at the time showed some 80% of the American public trusted the military; only 20% felt that way about the media.

General Colin L. Powell

1976 graduates from the National War College, promoted to colonel

1979 promoted to brigadier general while military assistant to the deputy secretary of defense

1983 promoted to major general while military assistant to the secretary of defense

1986 promoted to lieutenant general, commands Army Fifth Corps in Europe

1987 becomes assistant to the president for national security affairs

1989 promoted to general, sworn in as chairman of the Joint Chiefs of Staff on October 1. U.S. Senate approves a two-year extension of his chairmanship on October 1, 1991.

Decorations: as of 1991 include the DSM, 3DDSM, DSSM, 2LM, Soldier's Medal, BSM, PH, AM, JSCM, 3CR, CIB, Parachutist Badge, Pathfinder Badge, Ranger Tab.

Further Reading

Adelman, Ken. "Ground Zero: Colin Powell on War, Peace, and Balancing at the Center of Power," *The Washingtonian*, May 1990, p. 67.

Almond, Peter. "Gen. Powell Steps into Breach over Pentagon Budget," *The Washington Times*, October 2, 1989, p. A3.

Binder, L. James. "Gen. Colin L. Powell: 'If we're going to have a superpower sign outside our door, we've got to be ready to back it up'," *Army*, April 1990, p. 22.

Cannon, Lou. "Antidote to Ollie North," *The Washington Post Magazine*, August 7, 1988, p. W16.

Military Leaders Since World War II

Friedman, Saul. "Four-Star Warrior," *Long Island Newsday Magazine*, February 12, 1990, p. 10.

Rowan, Carl T. "Called to Service: The Colin Powell Story," *Reader's Digest*, December 1989, p. 121.

Wallechinsky, David. "'Have a Vision'," *Parade Magazine*, August 13, 1989, p. 4.

Weinberger, Caspar W. "General Colin Powell—An Inside View," *Forbes*, January 22, 1990, p. 31.

General Matthew B. Ridgway

Matthew B. Ridgway as Supreme U.S./U.N. Commander, Far East.
(National Archives)

*B*etween 1928 and 1933, Lieutenant Colonel George C. Marshall was in charge of instruction at the Army Infantry School, Ft. Benning, Georgia. Already a war veteran, Marshall implemented major changes in the school's field training exercises. He turned them from an outdoor walk-through of textbook lessons into a simulation of real combat. Student officers were given inaccurate maps, incomplete scouting reports, and ordered to make decisions quickly, on their own, while under mock attack.

Military Leaders Since World War II

Each year, in what he called "my little black book," Marshall wrote the names of those student-officers he thought had exceptional talent for acting quickly, "with good common sense." When Captain Matthew B. Ridgway graduated from the school's one-year advanced course in 1930, his name went into the "little black book."[1]

Self-reliance was not a talent Ridgway learned in 1930, at Ft. Benning. Since grade school, he had been taught to decide and act on his own. Born Matthew Bunker Ridgway on March 3, 1895, at Ft. Monroe, Virginia, the son of United States Military Academy graduate Thomas Ridgway, he grew up living the nomadic life typical of a career military officer's family. He entered grammar school in St. Paul, Minnesota and finished it in North Carolina. High school began in Virginia and ended in Massachusetts.

Much of his childhood was spent in the western United States, "back," he says, "when it really was the 'Wild West' of cowboys, Indians, and the Army." There, he learned from his father, on frequent hunting and camping trips, how to take care of himself in the open—"To bed down like the bear wherever nightfall might find me; to make myself at home in the mountains, on the prairie, the desert or the seashore." He also was taught a painful lesson in the use of weapons. "I had shot a farmer in the butt with my pellet-gun; and my father pounded into my head through the seat of my pants, *Never, ever* point a weapon at man or beast unless your intent is to kill them!'"

When he was 17, Ridgway pointed himself toward the United States Military Academy at West Point "at least as much because I felt it would please my father as because I had any burning desire to become a soldier." He flunked an exam (geometry) in 1912, on his first try for admission. He had to wait a year to try again, and this time he passed. He entered West Point in June 1913.

At the academy, he ached for one award more than any other: a varsity "A" in athletics. He never got it. "I was absolutely inept at all organized sports," he laughed many years later. His other failure, of sorts, was singing in the choir at Sunday church services. He enjoyed it—until he learned he could sleep an extra

---

[1] Another of the few names Marshall noted: Omar Bradley, first official chairman, in 1949, of the Joint Chiefs of Staff. Marshall did not list in his book those who failed to meet his standard because, he said snappily, "There wouldn't have been room."

General Matthew B. Ridgway

hour if he taught Sunday School instead. "The choir director didn't seem at all upset when I left."

Ridgway graduated on April 20, 1917, ranked 56th in a class of 139. Starting with the top-rated graduate, each newly commissioned second lieutenant is allowed to pick his first assignment. When "No. 56" reached the top of the list, no vacancies were left in his first choice, his father's artillery. So, he went with his second choice, the infantry. Two weeks later, he was with an infantry regiment along the U.S.–Mexican border in Texas.

On paper, Ridgway's Army record for the next 22 years reads pretty much like every other career officer's. He moved back and forth between field commands and staff jobs at some headquarters level. He went to school a lot: the Infantry School, the Army Command and General Staff College, the Army War College. And, like everybody else in the Army then, he waited a long time—15 years in his case—for a promotion.

Mostly due to his Spanish language skills, Ridgway drew some unusual assignments early in his career. He served, for instance, on a U.S. commission to referee Nicaraguan elections; on a U.S. board resolving border disputes between Bolivia and Paraguay; as an adviser to the governor general of the Philippine Islands; and, in 1939, on a team sent to Brazil to arrange basing rights for U.S. military ships and aircraft.

Back in that era, however, military diplomacy did not put many points on the career scoreboard. Neither did Ridgway's having spent six of his first seven Army years at West Point. Or did it? Ridgway began his tour there as assistant professor of Spanish and ended it as aide de camp to the academy superintendent. The superintendent was one of the Army's most renowned officers at the time, General Douglas MacArthur. His picking Ridgway to be his right-hand man was a strong vote of confidence—just as Marshall's notation in his "little black book" had singled out Ridgway for special notice earlier.

After the long, hard years, Ridgway finally saw a clear shot at top-level military leadership in late 1939. He was ordered to the Army General Staff's War Plans Division in Washington, D.C.— just as Marshall was sworn in as Army Chief of Staff. A war plans assignment, in Marshall's view, was a possible stepping stone to major combat command on the theory that, "You helped devise the plans; now, go execute them." For Ridgway, the move occurred in 1942.

Military Leaders Since World War II

First, he was assigned to the newly activated 82nd Infantry Division. By mid-year, it had been redesignated an Airborne Division and he had command of it. "Airborne" was a new idea in the Army then. It involved parachuting an entire combat division onto a battlefield from the air rather than marching it in overland.

"Ridgway got the 82nd Airborne started," says Jack Norton, a pioneer "Airborne guy" himself. "He organized it. He trained it. And he led it to a string of victories" in North Africa, Sicily, the Italian mainland, and the Allied landing at Normandy. When it was wedded to the newly formed XVIII Airborne Corps, he was the first commander of that, too; leading its record-setting charge across Belgium, France, and northern Germany. By mid-1945, Germany had surrendered.

Said a Legion of Merit citation Ridgway received midway through that cycle: Due to his "training and leadership," the 82nd "has become renowned for tactical skill; and the ability of each of its units, often widely separated in a landing area and in battle, to act, in the individual units and collectively, as a self-sufficient organization." Edward Rowny, himself an outstanding Army combat engineer during the war, says that, "Ridgway was easily one of the top five generals of World War II—and I include Eisenhower in that count."

Between 1946 and 1950, Ridgway's knack for military diplomacy was used in several places. He served, for instance, as one of the early U.S. delegates to the United Nations (UN) Military Staff Committee. He also helped in the early stages to create what officially became, in 1949, the North Atlantic Treaty Organization (NATO). NATO's initial 12 members included the United States, Canada, and Iceland, and all the countries of Western Europe except Spain. Basically, NATO was a military alliance designed to preserve stability in Europe by deterring Soviet territorial expansion.

Ridgway also played a brief, decisive role in 1946–47 organizing, as NATO's chairman, the Inter-American Defense Board. The board was then, and still is, the military arm of the Organization of American States (OAS). Essentially, the OAS is, for most of the countries of Central and South America, what NATO is for Europe: an alliance whose members promise to help each other resist invasion or subversion by outside forces.

After 1948, Ridgway was hidden in a Pentagon closet, as Army deputy chief of staff for administration. He had that "paper-clip-counting job," as Army folks call it, in June 1950, when the North

General Matthew B. Ridgway

Korean Communist army launched a massive attack on South Korea. A United Nations military force, comprised largely of Americans, was ordered to oust the invaders. General Douglas MacArthur, in Tokyo, was already wearing three hats: commander in chief, U.S. Far East Command; supreme commander, Allied Powers, Far East; and supervisor of the rebuilding of Japan's economy and the birth of its Allied-imposed political democracy. Now, he received an additional assignment: commander in chief of the United Nations military force.

In mid-December, the U.S. Eighth Army's commanding general, Walton H. Walker, was killed in a jeep accident. MacArthur called the Pentagon. He wanted Ridgway for the job. Ridgway reached the war zone on Christmas Day. Never had a general inherited more dismal prospects. For one thing, the UN political objective had been changed twice since June. The objective at first was to drive the North Korean army out of South Korea, thereby restoring South Korea's independence. After achieving that task, the UN forces were told to press forward into North Korea, with a view to reuniting the two countries into one. After massive Chinese forces came to the aid of North Korea in the counterattack of December 1951, the UN objective reverted to the restoration of South Korean independence.

In addition, the Joint Chiefs of Staff were lukewarm about reinforcing U.S. forces in Korea. They thought Korea was just a prelude to "the real Soviet attack" by the Red Army in Europe. Finally, Ridgway's immediate boss, MacArthur, and his ultimate one, President Truman, began to argue publicly, through Congress, over Korean War strategy and objectives. Until Walker's death, MacArthur had coached him in some detail on the combat tactics he wanted to see. When Ridgway arrived in Tokyo, MacArthur told him simply, "The Eighth Army is yours. Form your own opinion; make your own judgment. I will support you. I wash my hands of this Korean thing."

In Korea, Ridgway found, according to Edward Rowny, who was there, that "everybody was running to the rear to establish beachheads for evacuation to Japan." Ridgway summoned his staff and his corps commanders to a free-wheeling debate in a South Korean schoolhouse on a Sunday morning. The sum of the meeting was one corps commander, in charge of about 40% of Ridgway's combat forces, wanted to pull out; and the other corps commander wanted to stand, fight back, "and then go north." Ridgway took those two commanders into a side room.

Military Leaders Since World War II

When they returned, Ridgway announced to the assembly, "Gentlemen, we're going north."

"When word reached the troops," says Rowny, "he quickly was labeled, 'Wrong-way Ridgway'; but he was convinced they were good enough, they could stand, fight, and repel the enemy." With a string of aggressive attacks, some of which he led himself, Ridgway soon showed them they were far better than beatings by the Chinese had let them think they were. In April 1951, Truman fired MacArthur, and gave Ridgway all MacArthur's responsibilities.

By then, reported a *Time* magazine article, "Ridgway had turned the Eighth Army around [the main UN ground force in Korea at the time]. It was fighting back against Chinese and North

Ridgway (right) and MacArthur leave forward-area command post.
(National Archives)

16

General Matthew B. Ridgway

Korean communist forces three times its size and whipping them soundly. In one short period, it had inflicted an estimated 30,000 casualties on the enemy at small cost . . . and, in effect, had taken away a bargaining chip the Chinese were hammering at the UN, i.e. that 'our victory in Korea is inevitable.' "[2]

Before the end of the year, most of the Chinese combat forces had been pushed back up above the 38th parallel, the pre-war dividing line between North and South Korea. The Chinese, through their North Korean puppets, called for a truce conference. They had no real interest, yet, in a cease-fire, only in buying time to fortify their positions and to replace their combat losses. As the truce talks dragged on, the UN combat forces now were under a terrible strain.

Ordered by Washington to stay below the 38th parallel while under constant attack, they were being asked, basically, to risk their lives so UN negotiators under a tent near Panmunjom, Korea could "bargain from strength." This was a unique moment in American military history. Ridgway's ability to keep the fighting forces' morale high, in spite of their knowledge that they had been handed a "no-win" mission, was remarkable. Said Marshall, "Ridgway's campaign in Korea will be rated as a classic of personal leadership."

In May 1952, Ridgway was ordered to replace General of the Army Dwight D. Eisenhower as Supreme Commander, Allied Powers, Europe (SACEUR). Ridgway had no illusions about his NATO task being easy. He was replacing Dwight D. Eisenhower, "the personal embodiment of NATO itself, the eloquent salesman," said Ridgway, "who had persuaded [NATO] to agree on a common plan of mutual defense, to 'subscribe to the pretty magazine.' I was the so-and-so with the derby hat and cigar coming around at the first of the month to collect the [money]."

Concluded General Andrew Goodpaster, who would become SACEUR himself, "SHAPE was genuinely difficult for Ridgway. Many countries not only were not providing what they said they would provide to SHAPE. They were not even meeting their own obvious military needs." Ridgway, and even his wife, were attacked publicly and privately by all manner of people: KGB agents

---

[2]Treated almost as a footnote in general press coverage was Ridgway's order, in May 1951, for an immediate end to racial segregation in the Eighth Army. "It's un-American and un-Christian," he said, "and, besides, its inefficient."

in the French government, European editorial writers, angry government officials both in Europe and Washington.

They managed to create the impression that he had failed as SACEUR. That sour image stayed with him when he returned to the Pentagon in August 1953, to become Army Chief of Staff. The facts, however, don't fit the image. When he arrived in Europe, SHAPE had in it only the U.S. 1st Infantry Division, three light mechanized units, and a small British force. When he left, NATO had 15 war-ready divisions on active alert, two more in ready reserve—and he had received another Distinguished Service Medal for "dynamic leadership."

Ridgway's life in the Pentagon was no less troubled than his tour in Europe had been. His running fights were legion, particularly with then-Defense Secretary Charles E. Wilson, over where defense dollars were being spent. Growled Ridgway once, "The tendency, which was manifest many times during my tour, of civilian Secretaries making military decisions on the basis of political expediency constitutes a danger to this country."

One strong Ridgway objection was the "folly" of basing national security on "one military arm [the Air Force]" with a single weapon, the nuclear bomb. The idea of blasting cities into oblivion is, he said, "repugnant to the ideals of a Christian nation." Besides, he added, "The more primitive [Soviet] society is not a complex nerve fabric, a web of inter-related and interdependent functions and services as is ours. Spread nearly 6,000 miles from the Oder-Neisse in Europe to the Sea of Japan, [it] would be extremely difficult to destroy just as the turtle and the crocodile are harder to kill than the higher animals."

Vilified at the time, his arguments for strong, mobile, high-technology conventional combat forces would not begin to be funded until a decade after he retired. Ironically, by then even one of his "victories" as a military adviser to the president had been overturned.

During 1954 and 1955, Eisenhower was under pressure to send "a strong military force" into Indochina to fill the "power vacuum" left there by the North Vietnamese Communist's defeat of the French. Ridgway urged Eisenhower not to make that commitment. Armed with facts and figures, Ridgway concluded, "If we did go into Indochina, we would have to win. We could win but the cost in men and money would be as great as, or greater than, what we paid in Korea [33,746 killed in battle, 103,284 wounded]."

Eisenhower ended up agreeing with Ridgway. Support for Indochina continued to be the small band of military advisers first authorized by Truman in 1950. Noted Ridgway succinctly in 1956, "To the list of tragic accidents that fortunately never happened, I would add the [proposed] Indochina intervention."

Chronology

March 3, 1895	Matthew Bunker Ridgway born in Ft. Monroe, Virginia
1917	graduates from the U.S. Military Academy at West Point
1918–1924	serves as foreign language teacher, athletic director, and aide de camp at West Point
1929	completes 18 months' service on U.S. commissions to oversee Nicaraguan elections and to arbitrate a Bolivia-Paraguay border dispute
1932	promoted to major, his first promotion since he became a captain in 1917
1937	graduates from Army War College
1940–1945	promoted up through the ranks from lieutenant colonel to lieutenant general while commanding, most of that time, the 82nd Airborne Division, then the XVIII Airborne Corps, in Europe during World War II
1951	replaces General Douglas MacArthur as supreme commander of the United Nations Command in Korea and of the

	U.S. Command in the Far East, is promoted to general
1952	replaces General Dwight Eisenhower as supreme commander, Allied Powers, Europe
1953	becomes Army Chief of Staff
1955	retires from the Army to become chairman of the Mellon Institute of Industrial Research until 1960. He now divides his full retirement time between homes in Florida and Pittsburgh

Decorations: among the more than 60 U.S. and foreign-government medals he has received, personal decorations include 2DSC, 2SS, LM, 2BS, 4DSM, PH.

Further Reading

By Matthew Ridgway
The Korean War. Garden City, N.Y.: Doubleday, 1967 (in their Quality Paperbacks Series, 1986).

Soldiers: The Memoirs of Matthew B. Ridgway, as told to Harold H. Martin. New York: Harper & Brothers, 1956.

About Matthew Ridgway
Blair, Clay. *Ridgway's Paratroopers: The American Airborne in World War II.* Garden City, N.Y.: Dial Press, 1985.

"COMMAND: The Airborne General," *Time,* March 5, 1951, p. 26.

Condit, Doris M. *The Test of War: 1950–53.* Washington, D.C.: Historical Office of the Secretary of Defense, 1988. (Focus is on the Korean War but the book contains considerable detail on Ridgway.)

General Matthew B. Ridgway

Hackett, John L. *The General and the President: A Conflict in Strategies*. Carlisle Barracks, Pa.: U.S. Army War College, 1989.

"The Education of Matthew Ridgway," *The New York Times Magazine*, May 4, 1952, p. 7.

General William C. Westmoreland

General William C. Westmoreland.
(Official Army Chief of Staff photo)

---

*I*n 1982, a CBS-TV News team, called "CBS Reports," broadcast a 90-minute narration titled "The Uncounted Enemy: A Vietnam Deception." The program charged that "certain events . . . suggest a conspiracy at the highest levels of American military intelligence" in Saigon, South Vietnam, in 1967. As commander of the U.S. Military Assistance Command, Vietnam (MACV), General William C. Westmoreland had been the top field commander in Vietnam at the time.

The program claimed, basically, that he had ordered his people to hide from their civilian superiors in Washington the "fact" that "perhaps several hundred thousand" Communist North Vietnam-

General William C. Westmoreland

ese and Viet Cong guerrillas were assembling for an all-out assault on South Vietnam in January 1968. Though widely believed, the "CBS Reports" indictment was suspect on its face.

For one thing, Westmoreland didn't have the power to impose that kind of censorship. For another, combat commanders have a natural tilt toward overestimating, not underestimating, the size of an enemy force they're about to fight. Worst-case forecasts can lead to their being given more troops, more firepower; a rosy forecast can lead to high casualties and lost battles. In short, the CBS theme just didn't jibe with military common sense.

After the television show, General Andrew Goodpaster said, "Several of us asked him, 'Why the hell did you do that with those [CBS News] sharks?' He said it was 'because they told me it would be an opportunity for me to tell the story as it was.' And he believed they were honest about that." Added Army Lt. General Daniel O. Graham, one of the top intelligence and counter-intelligence officers in MACV in 1967, "Westy's biggest problem is he is the world's oldest living Boy Scout. He just cannot believe some people will lie to him."

Indeed, Westmoreland had been schooled all his life on some variation of the Military Academy motto, "Duty, Honor, Country." Born on March 26, 1914, in Saxon, Spartanburg County, South Carolina, he was christened William Childs Westmoreland. His mother, "Mimi" Childs, was from a South Carolina family prominent in state politics, textiles, railroading, banking, and was, as one Westmoreland biographer put it, "eminently solvent." His father, John Ripley Westmoreland, managed the Pacolet Mills textile plant in Spartanburg.

Westmoreland's American family heritage goes back to the 1740s when Thomas Westmoreland arrived in South Carolina with a 600-acre land grant given him by British King George II. Both his great-grandfather and grandfather had served with the South Carolina cavalry during the Civil War—during which five Westmorelands were killed. But the family heritage was in medicine and business, not the military. His mother wanted "Childs," as he was called in his youth, to become a doctor as his father's father had been. His father wanted him to become a lawyer.

However, his own choice began to take shape in 1929 when he was only 15. That year, he passed the last of the 21 merit-badge tests needed to become an Eagle Scout, the highest rank in the Boy Scouts. As a reward, his father paid his way to England to attend the Boy Scout World Jamboree, scouting's first such gath-

23

ering since the worldwide organization was founded there in 1910. For Westmoreland, he said later, the trip, "became a turning point in my life."

Altogether, his excursion lasted 70 days. He visited a good deal of Europe. In England he saw a cultural rainbow of teenage Boy Scouts from 74 countries. He also met in London a group of Navy midshipmen from Annapolis. The sum of it all was that Westmoreland decided law or medicine would have to wait a while. He was going to "Join the Navy and see the world!"

His father had graduated in 1900 from The Citadel, South Carolina's version of the Virginia Military Institute. An active benefactor of the school, "Rip" just assumed his only son would also go to college there. It was, after all, as good a spring-board into either medicine or law as any other college. After his European trip, "Childs" Westmoreland was no longer that committed to either following a career in medicine as his mother wanted, or law, as his father desired.

His application to The Citadel was helped some by his having been elected president of his high school senior class in 1931. On the other hand, he had been a particularly poor student in English composition. (He evaded flunking the course by creating, for the final exam, an exchange of letters between two poorly educated mountaineers—therefore, between two guys who, naturally, misspelled a lot of words.)

He entered The Citadel in fall 1931, adopting for himself his father's college nickname, "Rip." At the same time, he started pushing for permission to enter the U.S. Naval Academy. He pressed his father to ask James F. Byrnes, one of South Carolina's U.S. senators, to help. "Ask him, yourself," snapped his father, "you know him as well as I do." (Byrnes, the future secretary of state to President Harry S. Truman, had been young Westmoreland's (Episcopal) Bible class teacher.)

Westmoreland went to Byrnes but was advised to try the U.S. Military Academy instead. The courses there were less engineering-oriented, Byrnes claimed; and, with an Army officer's commission from West Point, he said, Westmoreland would be able to "see the world," anyway. Westmoreland took the suggestion. And, when the person Byrnes had initially nominated failed the entrance exams, Westmoreland, as Byrnes' first-alternate nominee, was accepted into West Point in July 1932.

His senior year, Westmoreland was first captain of the corps of cadets, the top student-officer rank at the academy. He graduated

General William C. Westmoreland

Westmoreland on one of his three- to four-times-a-week inspection trips.
(National Archives)

---

with the "Class of '36," ranked 151st in a class of 276. He also received, from famed World War I General John J. Pershing, the "Pershing Sword." That meant Westmoreland had been rated first in his class in military leadership and discipline.

Understandably, when Pershing spoke to the graduating class, his advice made a particularly strong impression on Westmoreland. Forty years later, he still remembered, "General Pershing [saying] decisiveness, initiative, determination, a concern for the individuality of your men, those were the essentials of leadership. Maintain your own morals at a high level, he said, and you will find them reflected in the morals of your men." And, Westmoreland added, "my own most rewarding experience of all" at West Point "was the appreciation and respect I gained for the Military Academy Code of Ethics, which its honor system exemplified: No lying, no cheating, no stealing, no immorality."

Westmoreland wanted to join the Army Air Corps, but he failed the physical exam because of a minor defect in his eyesight. So, he opted for the artillery, and was sent to a horse-drawn field artillery unit at Ft. Sill, Oklahoma. (The last horse-drawn active-duty Army field artillery battalion wasn't disbanded until mid-1942.) From there, in 1939, he went to the Eighth Field Artillery in Hawaii.

But, he still wanted an Air Corps commission. In Hawaii, he took flying lessons and qualified for a private pilot's license. He also strengthened his eyesight with a long, arduous set of prescribed exercises. However, by 1941, when he could have passed the Air Corps physical, Major Westmoreland was on his way to the 34th Field Artillery at Ft. Bragg, North Carolina, which one year later was on its way to war in North Africa. He decided he'd do the Army more good, for now, staying in the specialty where he was already well trained.

After the Allied victory in North Africa, the 82nd Airborne Division was the first Army outfit to land in Sicily. Lieutenant Colonel Westmoreland's artillery followed the next day. Westmoreland promptly tracked down the 82nd's commanding general, Matthew Ridgway, and volunteered his artillery to join Ridgway's forward elements. Ridgway managed the reassignment that day. One result was that Brigadier General Maxwell D. Taylor,[1] Ridgway's artillery commander, invited Westmoreland to dinner. And the result of that, in turn, was that artillery tactics Westmoreland had devised during the battle in North Africa soon were adopted by all the Army's artillery commands.

In March 1944, Westmoreland was executive officer of the Ninth Division Artillery when the division was moved to England. Following D-Day—the June 6, 1944, Allied invasion of France—Colonel Westmoreland was named division chief of staff. He

---

[1] A highly decorated paratrooper, himself, during World War II, Taylor, from 1955 through a portion of Westmoreland's 1964–68 tour as Commander of MACV, would be, variously, Army Chief of Staff, military advisor to President John F. Kennedy, chairman of the Joint Chiefs of Staff, and U.S. ambassador to South Vietnam.

General William C. Westmoreland

stayed there as the division fought its way across France, Belgium, and northern Germany to the end of the war. During that stretch, not authorized to fly Army observation planes—though he knew how—he had pilots constantly taking him up on reconnoitering missions. According to biographer Ernest B. Furgurson, when Westmoreland took off, his combat troops on the ground would tell each other, "Get ready; Westy is about to send us back to war again."

In Westmoreland's personnel records, still today, is an officer's comment: "He was all Army. He had no time for anything else. He never blew up. He told people what to do, and expected them to do it . . . There was no question he was one of the most patriotic, dedicated men I ever knew. We said he would become Chief of Staff of the Army one day, if he didn't stub his toe."

After the war, in May 1946, he was due to join the Operations and Planning Division (OPD) of the Army General Staff in the Pentagon—considered, at the time, a "star chance" for career advancement—but it was not to be. Major General James M. Gavin, now in command of the 82nd Airborne and another "Airborne" hero of World War II as Taylor and Ridgway had been, called Westmoreland to command one of Gavin's three regiments.

Thus, a 32-year-old colonel, whose age would have excused him from the test, went to jump school for a month. He graduated with not only a parachutist's badge but also a glider pilot's badge. Later, in what turned out to be preparation for his role in Vietnam, Westmoreland taught airborne and air mobile warfare, psychological warfare, and strategic planning for two years at the Army War College.

He remained a strong advocate of air mobile forces when he took command, in May 1952, of the 187th Airborne Combat Team in Korea. Then, and again in 1958, when he took command of the 101st Airborne Division, his training programs emphasized what he titled RECONDO, his acronym for "reconnaissance and commando."

As Ridgway had done earlier in many respects, Westmoreland's goal was to develop what he called "resourceful, independent-thinking, small-unit teams" expert in what today is called anti-terrorist, anti-guerrilla counterinsurgency. He installed the same training program at West Point when he was superintendent in 1960–63. He was not the first one to promote developing that kind of Army capability; but he certainly was among its early advocates.

Military Leaders Since World War II

His program also stressed another point that became very relevant to Vietnam: "Giving small tactical units clear information on what the job they're being ordered to risk their lives for is supposed to accomplish."

In between Korean and the 101st, Westmoreland held another key assignment, secretary of the Army General Staff. Basically, that meant he was chief of staff to the Army Chief of Staff who, during his three years there, was Maxwell Taylor. The job put Westmoreland center-stage in the endless contests between Army program ambitions and a swirl of essentially political opposition to them, both within the Pentagon and from higher, civilian authority outside the building.

Ridgway had warned, when he was Army Chief of Staff, that "civilian leaders should propose the *ends* that must be achieved and let the military leaders supply their estimate of how much [of those ends] can be attained by military *means* and how those *means* may be best employed." Westmoreland saw some transgressions of Ridgway's advice when he was working for Taylor in the Pentagon—and, later, in an epidemic of civilian and military superiors telling him, often in contradiction to each other, what he should do in Vietnam.

Few commanders in American history ever have been saddled with the twisted, tortured chain of command Westmoreland suffered. Even the formal "pecking order," as it was called, was complex. On the one hand, he reported to the commander in chief, Pacific Command, in Hawaii. That officer, usually an admiral, reported, in turn, to the Joint Chiefs of Staff, who reported to the secretary of defense.

On the other hand, because the war had so many foreign policy implications, he also reported to the State Department's ambassador in Saigon, who reported to the secretary of state, who reported only to the president, Westmoreland's top commander in chief. Beyond that, people in those two chains of command had no qualms, according to his memoirs, about ignoring the prescribed "pecking order."

As a result, during his tenure at MACV, he would get instructions from a member of the Joint Chiefs of Staff that, he learned later, his boss in Hawaii didn't know about. He would get orders from his commander in chief or the secretary of defense that, he learned, even his contacts on the Joint Chiefs of Staff didn't know about.

In addition, he had to cope with a conflict within his own ranks. On the one hand, there were those subordinates who wanted to

General William C. Westmoreland

concentrate on the guerrilla war, i.e., fight the terrorists in the local hamlets and, at the same time, teach the local population how to defend itself. On the other hand, there were those who, like Westmoreland, wanted to attack and destroy the conventional North Vietnamese military forces—the primary source of the war in the first place.

Westmoreland at his preferred site for talking to the troops, on the hood of a jeep.
(Official U.S. Army photo)

Ultimately, however, the problem wasn't with the tactics, but in the strategic plan. On the one hand, as in Korea 25 years earlier, the mission ordered by Presidents John F. Kennedy and Lyndon B. Johnson, Secretary of State Dean Rusk, and Secretary of

Defense Robert S. MacNamara, among others in Washington, was to use military force to stop the North Vietnamese government from using military force to dominate its neighbors, South Vietnam, Laos, and Cambodia. That's the war Westmoreland was waging.

On the other hand, North Vietnam's leaders, as they later confessed, were fighting an essentially psychological war for political and economic control over all Indochina (the name for Laos, Cambodia, and Vietnam while they were a French colony from, roughly, 1862 until 1954). Thus, given their objective, their definition of "war" included the use of not only military force, but also propaganda and diplomatic negotiations.

Summed up by Westmoreland, in a February 1990 edition of *Vietnam* magazine, "[Their] objective was to defeat the *will* [Westmoreland's emphasis] of the United States . . . And, indeed, that is exactly what they did. The United States was defeated psychologically, politically and diplomatically by a clever enemy. It was not defeated on the military battlefield."

The most highly publicized proof of Westmoreland's claim occurred in the so-called Tet offensive of late-January to mid-February 1968 in South Vietnam. (The Tet holiday, which begins on January 29 means to all Vietnamese what Christmas and New Years mean to Americans.) The offensive began on January 21 with a diversionary attack by North Vietnamese regulars on a strong U.S. military outpost in the South Vietnamese central highlands.

Then, beginning on the eve of Tet, January 28, and over the next two days, a total force of approximately 85,000 mostly Viet Cong "irregulars", i.e., guerrillas, attacked targets, almost simultaneously, in 36 of South Vietnam's 44 provinces, five of her six autonomous cities, 64 of her 242 district capitals, and 50 hamlets. The Tet offensive was a North Vietnamese victory psychologically. According to opinion polls taken later that year, more than half the American public strongly opposed U.S. military combat in Vietnam.

Measured on a strictly military scale, however, Tet was an absolute disaster for the North Vietnamese. Within two weeks after the offensive began, more than 40% of the attacking force (37,000 troops) had been killed, 5,800 captured, and the rest, most of them wounded, had fled to sanctuaries in Laos and Cambodia. (Total American, South Vietnamese, and other allied losses were 3,000 killed—plus 3,000 civilians executed by

General William C. Westmoreland

North Vietnamese troops in the South Vietnamese provincial capital of Hue.) The Viet Cong were never again a factor in the war.

A year after Tet, North Vietnam's top commander, General Vo Nguyen Giap, admitted to an Italian journalist, Oriana Fallaci, that, between 1964 and 1969, he had lost more than 500,000 soldiers killed in battle plus uncounted thousands more missing or permanently crippled. Yet, in 1975 in Hanoi, when a U.S. Army historian, Colonel Harry Summers, reminded a North Vietnamese officer, "You know, you never beat us on the battlefield," the North Vietnamese officer answered, "That may be so, but it is also irrelevant."

Such ambiguities and ironies as that about the Vietnam War make it very difficult to judge Westmoreland's overall performance there. When he assumed command of MACV in 1964, South Vietnam was on the verge of military and political collapse. When he left in 1968 to become Army Chief of Staff (until 1972 when he retired), American forces were the most expert in the world at fighting the military phase of what is called "counterinsurgency warfare."

But, by the end of his military career, "Westy," as he was called, had become a scapegoat, a symbol of a crusade gone sour. Given that circumstance alone, it likely will be many years before an objective assessment of his contributions to military leadership can emerge.

Chronology

March 26, 1914	William Childs Westmoreland born in Spartanburg, South Carolina
1936	graduates from the U.S. Military Academy
1942–1945	commands or is on headquarters staff of artillery and infantry battalion, regimental and division combat units in North Africa, and Europe during World War II; promoted from captain in 1940 to colonel in 1944

1947	after passing paratrooper course and commanding a parachute-infantry regiment, becomes 82nd Airborne Division chief of staff
1950	assigned as professor at, first, the Army Command and General Staff College; then, the Army War College
1952–1953	commands Airborne regimental combat team during Korean War and is promoted to brigadier general
1955–1958	serves as secretary of the Army General Staff in the Pentagon with promotion to major general
1963	promoted to lieutenant general and transferred from being superintendent of the U.S. Military Academy to being commander of both the Strategic Army Command and its XVIII Airborne Corps
1964–1968	promoted to general and commands U.S. Military Assistance Command, Vietnam (MACV)
1968–1972	serves as Army Chief of Staff; has lived in Spartanburg since his 1972 retirement

Decorations: his more than 50 medals, citations, and badges include 3DSM, 3LM, 2BSM, 9AM, CIB.

Further Reading

By William Westmoreland
A Soldier Reports. Garden City, N.Y.: Doubleday, 1976.

General William C. Westmoreland

"As I saw it and now see it: A perspective on America's unique experience in Vietnam," *Vietnam*, February 1990, p. 62.

"The long haul, with an escape route," *The Washington Times*, October 8, 1990, p. G-1.

About William Westmoreland

Adler, Renata. *Reckless Disregard: Westmoreland v. CBS, et. al.* New York: Knopf Publishers, distributed by Random House, 1986.

Brewin, Bob and Sydney Shaw. *Vietnam on Trial: Westmoreland vs. CBS.* New York: Atheneum, 1987.

Furgurson, Ernest B. *Westmoreland: The Inevitable General.* Boston: Little, Brown & Co., 1968.

Kowet, Don. *A Matter of Honor.* New York: Macmillan, 1984.

"Man of the Year" (1965), *Time*, January 7, 1966, p. 15.

Palmer, General Bruce, Jr. *The 25-Year War: America's Military Role in Vietnam.* Lexington, Ky.: University of Kentucky Press, 1984.

Roth, M. Patricia. *The Artist and the General.* New York: Morrow, 1986.

General Creighton W. Abrams

Abrams, with his ever-present cigar, on an aerial reconnaissance mission over South Vietnam.
(National Archives)

When Creighton William Abrams, Jr., was 12 years old, his parents bought him and his two younger sisters, ages 9 and 10, a puppy. It was about the only luxury the family could afford during Abrams' childhood. After the dog was brought home, an argument erupted between the two girls over who would take care of it. "Creighton will take care of it," their mother announced firmly, "because I know if Creighton is supposed to do it, it will be done."

During the last decade of his life, 1964–1974, General Creighton Abrams was assigned to "take care of" one of the most frustrating sets of tasks given any American military leader since World War II: the Vietnam War. He was not the only one in charge, however, which was part of the problem. Another serious obstacle he faced was a series of political decisions back home which severely restrained his combat options. "We were like a boxer in a prizefight," said one of Abrams' predecessors. "Every time we'd beat the other guy into the ropes, our managers [in the Pentagon, White House, or Congress] would throw in the towel."

Between 1964 and 1967, as Army vice chief of staff, Abrams' main responsibility was to direct a massive buildup of Army forces in Vietnam. That sharply increased commitment had been triggered, in turn, by the Gulf of Tonkin Resolution. Enacted in August 1964, at President Lyndon Johnson's insistence, with a nearly unanimous supporting vote in Congress, the resolution was only a step short of being an open declaration of war against North Vietnam.

The plain-language translation of what the resolution said was that, if North Vietnamese forces attacked U.S. forces "in Southeast Asia," U.S. forces were authorized to counterattack—including aerial bombing assaults on supply bases in North Vietnam. In effect, the resolution opened the way for the transfer of combat responsibilities from the South Vietnamese to the Americans.

Abrams' job, assembling and deploying those U.S. forces, "was made infinitely more difficult," says his biographer, Dr. Lewis Sorley, "by President Lyndon Johnson's refusal to call up the National Guard and Reserves, which all Pentagon contingency plans assumed would be used." (Those plans still do, as was proved when large numbers of reserves were part of the U.S. military deployment to the Persian Gulf in 1991.)

Another problem wrapped around Abrams' mission was what the Pentagon's civilian leadership of that era called "systems analysis." Essentially, it was the use of computer-driven arithmetic to produce what its advocates, including the then-Secretary of Defense Robert S. McNamara, claimed would be more "cost-effective" solutions to military problems. Over-used, as it often was in that era, it amounted to an accountant's statistics over-ruling military judgment based on experience.

Abrams once highlighted very simply how systems analysis could hide a top-level Pentagon decision-maker from the real world of combat. McNamara's systems analysts had spent a morning meeting contesting the size of the Army buildup Abrams planned for Vietnam. Back in his office, Abrams announced, "Well, I now understand what 'Systems Analysis' means. In the next war, the last remaining American shoots and kills the last remaining Russian; then his rifle falls apart and his uniform turns to rags and falls off his back; and we will all say proudly, 'We have fought a cost-effective war.' "

Abrams spent the next year (1968) as deputy commander, U.S. Military Assistance Command, Vietnam (MACV), and the following three as commander, MACV. There, he inherited an additional set of burdens. One was very basic. In 1964–65, the Joint Chiefs of Staff had developed war plans for Vietnam that followed a long-standing military doctrine: "Go in hard and fast with a clearly overwhelming military force." For nearly six years, in most cases, they were refused permission to use the tactics their plans recommended.

Specifically, their request to mine North Vietnam's Haiphong Harbor, to prevent Soviet ships from supplying the North Vietnamese with war material, was allowed only once, briefly, in 1972. Their proposal to bomb North Vietnam's military warehouses and transportation terminals "back into the Stone Age," as then-Air Force Chief of Staff Curtis LeMay put it, was denied. Instead, bombing raids on North Vietnam were allowed only sporadically, and top Pentagon civilians selected most of the targets. Permission was given only once to attack the Ho Chi Minh Trail in Laos and Cambodia, a 5,000-mile network of roads which was Hanoi's main supply line to its combat forces in South Vietnam. Even then, Congress forbade Abrams, by then commander, MACV from using U.S. ground forces in the mission and the secretary of defense denied him the use of U.S. aircover to support the South Vietnamese troops who did attack.

Lieutenant General Jack Norton, commander of the 1st Air Cavalry Division for a time before Abrams' arrival in Vietnam, said afterwards, "We were winning battles by big margins. But we knew, if we couldn't hit the Ho Chi Minh Trail, couldn't go after Hanoi, we couldn't win the war. We waited two years [1965–66] for the same order Ridgway had given us in 1950, 'Gentlemen, let's go North.' We never got that order. We couldn't believe it." (The order wasn't forthcoming for political reasons. American policymakers in Washington feared an all-out U.S. war effort might result in a direct U.S. military confrontation with China, or the Soviet Union, or both.)

Abrams had said once that, "Soldiering is an affair of the heart." Needless to say, all the restrictions placed on him in Vietnam were a terrible drain on his troops' morale. Indeed, one of the really amazing aspects of the no-win Vietnam conflict was that deser-

General Creighton W. Abrams

Abrams telling a two-star what he expects on a mission.
(National Archives)

---

tions and mental breakdowns occurred far less often in Vietnam between August 1964 and January 1973 (when the last U.S. combat forces left Vietnam), than had occurred in either the "no-win" Korean War or World War II.

That was doubly surprising because everyone in the field knew that with the election of a new president, Richard M. Nixon, in 1968, and the appointment of a new secretary of defense, Melvin R. Laird, in 1969, that the rules of engagement, as the military calls them, had been changed—slightly. Abrams was given two specific "top-priority" instructions: Train and equip the South Vietnamese to defend themselves; and "Get our combat people out of Vietnam where we shouldn't have been in the first place."

The first task looked nearly impossible when connected to the two-year withdrawal timetable for the second. It wasn't that the South Vietnamese soldiers and pilots were too inept to learn; rather it was simply that their training had not been the U.S. forces' first priority until then. The U.S. combat commitment had gone from 16,000 American military "advisers" when Westmoreland went to Saigon in January 1964, to more than 300,000 U.S. military personnel in Vietnam when Abrams arrived there in 1967. About 60% of those were in combat forces' supply-and-logistics pipeline.

While they had been doing most of the fighting, the South Vietnamese forces were being used by their own generals (who also were the governors of the country's 44 provinces and/or the "mayors" of the nation's cities) mostly to guard the generals and the cities where they lived. In addition, beginning in 1963, the coup d'etat had become almost routine in the dictatorial Vietnamese central government. Consequently, neither the mostly rural population nor Vietnam's ARVN (Army of the Republic of South Vietnam) leaders had any great loyalty or affection for a government which seemed to change as often as the weather.

Either of these tasks, troop training and troop withdrawal, would have been burden enough for one military leader. Adding to the strain was all the "help" Abrams received from a hostile press and what one observer called the "eager beavers" back in the Pentagon and the White House. Abrams handled the journalists with masterful understanding. Westmoreland had worked very hard on press relations, holding frequent, formal press conferences. All it got him was a drumbeat of editorial criticism which rumbled on well past his retirement from the Army. Abrams didn't hold any press conferences at all while he was commander, MACV. "Arguing with the press," he told one of his staff officers, "is like wrestling with a hog. You're both going to get filthy; and they're going to love it." So, Abrams simply talked to them alone, one at a time, wherever he found one. For the press, it was "an ego trip," and "exclusive interview" they could brag about to their bosses back in the United States. As a result, in their stories, Abrams was always noted as "one of the good guys."

Abrams' other obstacle, the "eager beavers," weren't so easy to handle. Noted General Bruce Palmer, "There was a lot of infighting going on back in Washington. For instance, the White House military adviser to the president poached on the secretary of state's territory. The president, himself, often made decisions normally reserved for the chairman of the Joint Chiefs. Abrams received orders directly from the secretary of defense or the White House as well as those issued through regular military channels (as also had been done to Westmoreland)."

"The instructions often were conflicting, the messages contradictory," said Palmer, "and always marked 'Urgent, from Wash-

General Creighton W. Abrams

Westmoreland, shirt sleeves rolled up, greets Army Vice Chief of Staff Abrams on arrival at Tan Son Nhut airport, Saigon.
(National Archives)

---

ington.'" A lover of classical music, Abrams coped with the chaos, Palmer reported, "by playing Wagnerian operas, particularly the wild strains of '*Ride of the Valkyries*,'[1] at full volume very late into the evening in his quarters while sipping scotch and water. That helped him maintain his sanity."

"The very dicey task," as Palmer called it, "of disengaging American troops from a war not over was a challenge to troop leadership unparalleled in our history." It was a measure of Abrams' "professionalism" and "great wartime leadership," thinks Palmer, that Abrams handled the task "without generating any serious disciplinary or morale problems." The single most impressive test result of Abrams' training program was turned in by the South Vietnamese seven months before Abrams was sworn in as Army Chief of Staff.

---

[1] In Germanic mythology, the Valkyries were the maidens of the God, Odin. They chose the heroes to be slain in battle; then led them to the paradise of Valhalla.

Military Leaders Since World War II

On March 30, 1972, a year after nearly all U.S. Army and Marine Corps combat forces had been withdrawn from Vietnam, a North Vietnamese multi-division force of infantry, tanks, and artillery launched a three-pronged assault across South Vietnam's northern and western borders.[2] Rather quickly, the South Vietnamese, supported by U.S. air power and military advisers on the ground, shredded the spearheads. In the end, North Vietnam suffered more than 100,000 casualties (an estimated 20–25% of its army), and lost most of its tanks and artillery. And North Vietnam's chief general, Vo Nguyen Giap, was fired by Hanoi.

Palmer, who was in the same West Point graduating class as both Westmoreland and Abrams, and whose Army career paralleled both of theirs to a great extent, once likened the personalities and leadership styles of the two to those of Confederate General Robert E. Lee and Union General Ulysses S. Grant—the coolly reserved, aristocratic Southerner, cautiously calculating vs. the tough-talking, hot-tempered, demanding, yet drink-up-with-the-boys Northerner from the poor side of town.

That Lee vs. Grant analogy is not entirely accurate. Abrams was born in Massachusetts, the son of a railroad mechanic. "They were a poor but happy family," says Abrams' biographer Sorley. Most of the family's food was grown in their own backyard garden; and the largest room in the tiny house where they lived was only nine feet square.

Abrams' one outstanding success in high school was being named captain of the football team. That earned him a small scholarship offer from Brown University; but the cost of his room, board, and books would have to come from Abrams, and his family didn't have the money. Then, he heard a professor from a nearby town extolling to his class one day the "great" educational opportunities at the U.S. Military Academy—and the fact that the Army paid for most them itself. With the help of three elderly school teachers coaching him every night after high school class, he passed the entrance exams and, when two people ahead of him on the nominating list failed, he was accepted into West Point in 1932.

Says General Andrew Goodpaster, who entered the Academy three years later and sat for a year at the same football-training table as Abrams during meals, "At West Point, Abe was not distinguished for his discipline." Again, he was popular and a

---

[2]Abrams had predicted within one day when the 1972 North Vietnamese assault would happen.

General Creighton W. Abrams

tough, aggressive lineman on the football team. But, whereas Westmoreland graduated with honors for "military proficiency," Abrams graduated 185th in the same class of 276. In short, Abrams kept rather well hidden during those years what Lieutenant General DeWitt C. Smith, Jr., later would call Abrams' "moral and physical courage, dignity, strength, sense of humor, total integrity and great wisdom—above all, integrity and wisdom."

After graduation, Abrams spent his first four years in the infantry. Then, in 1940, he "joined the armored force," as the military say, and all those characteristics Smith would mention later began to surface. During World War II, he earned a batch of medals and one remarkable bit of praise. Said his famous World War II commander, General George S. Patton, Jr., "I'm supposed to be the best tank commander in the Army; but I have one peer—Abe Abrams. He's the world's champion."

Abrams' talents showed up again in Germany in 1961 when Abrams commanded the Third Armored Division and Goodpaster the Eighth Infantry Division. "There were a lot of administrative duties," says Goodpaster, "and a lot of joint-operations planning. It was a great opportunity for disagreement. Abe's performance was superb. Under a rather gruff exterior, he had one of the keenest minds for military plans; a remarkable sense of combat action . . . The Army rightly named its main battle tank after him."[3]

Abrams was in a national spotlight in 1962–63. He was working in the Army General Staff's G-3 (Operations) office in the Pentagon during the fall of 1962 when Mississippi's state governor blocked an attempt by African-American James Meredith to enroll in the University of Mississippi. The following year, the governor of Alabama, George Wallace, and local police in Birmingham tried the same maneuver against black children trying to enter a formerly all-white grade school there. In both cases, President John F. Kennedy ordered a U.S. Army riot-control team in to enforce the students' rights.

When the military is ordered to restore order in domestic conflicts, the Army Chief of Staff is required to put a personal representative on site. Abrams got the assignment both times; and both times, Abrams was praised for handling tactfully but firmly a potentially explosive crisis. Along the way, he also "handled" a

---

[3] Goodpaster's reference is to the M-1A1 "Abrams" tank. A high-technology "star" of the five-week war against Iraq in 1991, it was roughly 20 years in development; but is, today, reputedly, the most combat-capable tank in the world.

Military Leaders Since World War II

president and an attorney general. First, at Birmingham, President Kennedy called Abrams and told him to move a platoon of troops to a particular place. Abrams, whose professional candor was well known, refused the order, telling the president, "The troops are exactly where they should be."

While Abrams was talking to President Kennedy, according to Abrams' aide, "Bobby Kennedy called." After being told that Abrams was busy, "Bobby yelled, 'Tell Abrams this is the Attorney General of the United States of America; and I want to talk to Abrams right now!" Given the message, Abrams' well-documented temper erupted. He skewered his aide with a glare and snapped, "Tell the kid I'm talking to his brother!" (President Kennedy later called back to apologize for giving Abrams a hard time.)

Said Palmer of his classmate, "Sometimes he only pretended anger, chewing on his ever present cigar, deliberately showing his blood pressure was up before he exploded. One never knew, however, whether it was an act or whether he had, in fact, lost his temper—and most people did not want to find out. Practically speaking, whether it was an act or for real made little difference. He got the results he wanted."

Abrams' job pressures did not ease when he became Army Chief of Staff in October 1972. Even before 1973, when the North Vietnamese signed a peace treaty with South Vietnam—one whose provisions they immediately began to violate—Congress declared a "peace dividend." It translated simply into a shift of federal spending from defense to a spate of domestic programs—launching a flood of red ink that has continued ever since.

For Abrams, that meant cutting forces and firing people. In its way, it was as hard on morale as the tough choices he had had to make in Vietnam in 1970–71 over which combat forces could go home. Then, in 1974, Congress stopped all military aid to Southeast Asia. That decision destroyed morale in the South Vietnam army. Holding its own in battle up to that point, it caved in. And then, on September 4, 1974 Abrams died of cancer at the Walter Reed Army Medical Center in Washington, D.C.

Wrote Palmer a decade later, "The hard thought lingers that, . . . had Abrams lived, would he have been able to persuade the Congress and the American people to go to [South Vietnam's] rescue? Abrams had a 'father-savior-hero' image in Vietnam. But . . . because the Presidency was [now] paralyzed [by the Watergate scandal] maybe even an Abrams could not have overcome such an obstacle."

Chronology

September 15, 1914	Creighton William Abrams, Jr. born in Springfield, Massachusetts
1936	graduates from the U.S. Military Academy
1944	becomes a tank battalion commander, leading General George S. Patton's Third Army into France, Belgium and, finally, Germany to help end World War II
1946	becomes chief of the Tactics Department, Armored School, Ft. Knox, Kentucky
1953	after promotion to colonel, becomes, chief of staff of, successively, three different Army corps in Korea
1956	promoted to brigadier general while chief of staff, the Armored Center, Ft. Knox, Kentucky
1960	promoted to major general and given an armored division command in Germany
1962	is assigned to the office, deputy chief of staff for operations, Department of the Army in the Pentagon
1963	becomes a lieutenant general in command of a corps in Germany
1964	promoted to general, named U.S. Army vice chief of staff
1968	becomes commander, U.S. Military Assistance Command, Vietnam (MACV)
1972	sworn in as Army Chief of Staff

1974 dies of cancer at Walter Reed Army Medical Center

Decorations: in addition to the more than three dozen unit citations and foreign-government medals he received, awards to him personally include 4DSMs, DDSM, 2DSCs, 2LMs, 2 Silver Stars and a BSM for valor.

Further Reading

By Creighton Abrams
Abrams, Lt. Col. Creighton W. "Armor in the Team," *Armor*, May-June 1985, p. 31.

About Creighton Abrams
Buckley, Kevin P. "General Abrams Deserves a Better War," *The New York Times Magazine*, October 5, 1969, p. 34.

Cochran, Alexander S., Jr. "The Tragic Commander," *Vietnam*, December 1989, p. 22.

Laird, Melvin R. "Unforgettable Creighton Abrams," *Reader's Digest*, July 1976, p. 72.

Langguth, A. J. "General Abrams Listens to a Different Drum," *The New York Times Magazine*, May 5, 1968.

McArthur, George. "Gen. Abrams Provides His Own Epitaph," *The Los Angeles Times*, September 5, 1974.

Sorley, Dr. Lewis. *Thunderbolt: General Creighton Abrams and the Army of His Times*. New York: Simon & Schuster, 1992.

General Edward L. Rowny

Official portrait of Edward L. Rowny as Army lieutenant general.
(National Archives)

Between 1955 and 1959, when he was halfway through his 51-year career in public service, then-Colonel Edward Leon Rowny worked as, first, deputy to, then chief of staff for, Supreme Headquarters Allied Powers Europe (SHAPE), the military arm of the North Atlantic Treaty Organization (NATO), the most important alliance among the Western industrialized nations since the end of World War II. Rowny's experience there inspired him to return to school to earn (in 1977) a Ph.D in international studies from American University.

His doctoral thesis was on decision-making in large, complex organizations such as NATO and the U.S. Defense Department. Decisions to be made in NATO, he wrote, or the Pentagon, or nearly every other kind of organization for that matter, come in three categories: Category 1—the relatively easy ones are the decisions which have to be made in times of crisis; Category 2—more difficult to make are decisions which change an organization's basic strategy; Category 3—the third, and most difficult, decisions to make involve changing the organization itself when events and trends in its world argue it must if it is to survive.

Decisions in Category 1 usually are up to a single individual, usually have to be made quickly (as in combat, for instance), and, like tests in school, produce a result just as quickly. Category 2 and 3 decisions take longer, both to reach and to pay off. One reason for that is inertia. Large organizations are like giant, ocean-going oil tankers. They simply can't zip off in new directions as easily as a sailboat.

In addition, creative decision-makers regularly are frustrated by fierce headwinds. A change in strategy can mean a change in who gets to go first to Congress for funding. A change in the organization, itself, can mean putting some people out of work—including even those who agree that the change is necessary. Rowny spent the last half of his career working mostly in that risky environment of Category 2 and 3 issues.

The most publicized of his work was his 17 years spent in arms reduction negotiations with the Soviet Union—first, as Lt. General Rowny, representative of the Joint Chiefs of Staff, and, later, as Ambassador Rowny. He also was a principal player in changing NATO's war-prevention strategies, and, again, in making gains in both the firepower and mobility of Army combat forces. Every one of those was as threatening to his career as his combat commands in World War II and Korea had been.

To some extent, the reasons Rowny was ordered, or simply felt required, to be a part of those issues can be traced back to his teenage years. His father had come to Baltimore, Maryland from Poland in 1912 at age 19 with a high school diploma and a menial "go-fer" job in Baltimore Harbor. But, shortly after Ed Rowny was born in 1917, his father had earned an architectural draftsman's degree, by attending night school, and launched the G. John Rowny construction company.

When Ed Rowny was six, his mother, whose parents also were Polish immigrants, became so ill she would not recover for ten years. So, until Rowny graduated from high school (at age 16), he and his baby brother were raised by his father and maternal grandmother. His early years weren't devoted solely to excelling in school. He also developed what friends today call "a world-class talent," playing the harmonica. (Larry Adler, who did become a world-famous harmonica virtuoso in the 1940s, received his first lessons from Rowny—though, in his biography, he gives Rowny no credit for his start.)

In 1933, Rowny enrolled in Baltimore's Johns Hopkins University. His plan was to earn a civil engineering degree (which he did, in 1937), and then help his father expand the construction company. Rowny changed his mind about the construction company in 1936. In Europe for summer studies at a Polish university, on a Kosciusko Foundation scholarship,[1] he also toured the continent. In Berlin for the 1936 Olympic Games, he was shaken by the "grim, goose-stepping Nazi youth," the "fanatic cheering" of organized mobs. "It was clear to me," he said, "that war was coming."

So, in July 1937, after graduating from Johns Hopkins, the 20-year-old Rowny resigned a commission he had earned there in the Army Engineers' Reserve; and he got himself into the U.S. Military Academy. Notes Lieutenant General Jack Norton, himself a member of that West Point Class of '41, "Rowny already was an honors graduate from Johns Hopkins. He spent most of his library time at 'the Point' just reading good books." Still, all Rowny's free-time activity, from track team to chess club, was noted more for energy than achievement. The one exception was that his debating team won the 1940 United States National Championship.

Then in 1941, his career nearly aborted. His eyesight suddenly went bad, from 20/20 to 20/200, for some still unknown reason. At graduation, he wouldn't receive a commission if his eyesight was worse than 20/100. Major George Lincoln (nicknamed "Abe," of course), his political science instructor, paid to send him to an eye doctor in New York City. The result was months of eye exercises and no reading at all. He did squeak through the eye test—and "no-reading Rowny" still graduated 59th in his class of 424.

Following graduation, he was sent to a combat engineers training outfit. From there until the end of World War II in Italy, Rowny became known, to quote General Robert Porter, as "very young [in his mid-20s], but very able, very active," in a variety of military skills from combat command to headquarters staff work. His commanding officers pulled him along with them when they were transferred from one command to another. His last commanding officer in Italy, on VE (Victory in Europe) Day in May 1945, became chief of General Douglas MacArthur's military staff in

---

[1]Polish general, military engineer, and patriot Thaddeus Kosciusko, 1746–1817, fought with American forces in the Revolutionary War.

Military Leaders Since World War II

Japan in 1949, and he summoned Rowny to join him. And in 1952, when the commander of the 2nd Infantry Division in Korea became commandant of the Infantry School, Ft. Benning, Georgia, he took his three regimental commanders, including Rowny, with him.

While in the Far East, Rowny increased his collection of combat medals. He also helped create what is called today the Japanese Self-Defense Force. In addition, he helped plan the Inchon landing that turned the tide of the Korean War in the United Nations' favor, at least for a while.

In the meantime, in 1945–47, after his commander in Italy had finally, reluctantly, allowed him to leave, Rowny was in the Pentagon, part of the strategic plans section of the Army General Staff's Operations and Plans Division (OPD). The section, headed by Rowny's former West Point mentor, now Brigadier General "Abe" Lincoln, called themselves "Abe's Brigade." Twelve key players in all, they were a powerhouse, both in influence and intellect. Half had been Rhodes scholars as had Lincoln. One, Dean Rusk, would become secretary of state.

December 1950 in Korea, Lieutenant Colonel Rowny receives Legion of Merit from Major General Edward M. Almond, X Corps commander.
(U.S. Army photo)

48

General Edward L. Rowny

They were the heart of OPD which, in turn, had been, during World War II and continued to be after the war, the heart of the Army General Staff. They worked mostly on Category 2 and 3 kinds of problems. For the Army Chief of Staff, they devised war goals and strategies, and they were his principal staff contact with the White House and the fledgling Joint Chiefs of Staff. Shortly after Rowny arrived, his friend "Abe" Lincoln, returned to teach at West Point, a move which required demotion to colonel.

The new leader Rowny acquired, as head of OPD, was Air Force Brigadier General Lauris Norstad. He promptly got the attention of "Abe's Brigade" when he began to hold regularly what he called "dream" sessions. They intrigued "Abe's Brigade." Says Rowny, "We worked hard preparing for those, reading history, talking to scientists, to global strategists, to heads of 'think tanks.'" Among the "dreams" he can recall their having in 1946-47: submarine-launched ballistic missiles; what today is called the space shuttle; and a detailed plan "to put a man on the Moon within 25 years."

Without a game plan, arguments about the cost of defense, about who should play what position on the team, are pointless. For exactly that reason, one of the stormiest national security issues was (and is) the argument over basic military strategy. On one side have been those who believed an enemy, meaning the Soviet Union, would not start World War III if it knew the reaction would be a hailstorm of nuclear bombs from U.S. air power. The opposition to that strategy has called it "madness." Security, they insist, requires, in addition to air power, strong armies and navies. Only those, they contend, can project conventional military power across the oceans to stop a "little war" before it escalates into a nuclear one.

Air power won the first round. Air Force General Norstad did not like the decision. Not until the mid-1950s, however—after Norstad became Supreme Allied Commander, Europe (SACEUR), and brought Rowny over as his chief of staff—did NATO begin to shift its strategy from "massive nuclear retaliation" to one that balanced Army, Navy, and Air force power in a "strategy of flexible response." And not until 1962 was the strategy of flexible response accepted as basic Pentagon doctrine—its advocates having suffered dozens of career casualties in the process. And not until about 1970 were sufficient combat forces trained, equipped, and deployed to do what the "new" strategy said they should be able to do.

During most of Rowny's career spent on that issue, he also was promoting another major change in military organization and combat strategy. Today, the Army brags about its helicopter-borne air cavalry. But, for Rowny, melding an air cavalry into Army tactics, organization, and equipment took 15 years of debate. It was as bitterly contested as the flexible response strategy had been. His promotion of air cavalry often grated on the traditional Army chain of command. (Compared to that stress, Rowny's overloaded two years, 1947–49, earning master's degrees in both engineering and international relations at Yale University, seemed a cakewalk.)

For instance, in 1961–62, he was both an assistant commander of the 82nd Airborne Division, and director of tests for its parent, the XVIII Airborne Corps. In effect, Rowny could overrule the commander of the 82nd if he needed its troops, which he usually did, for large-scale field tests, using helicopters for infantry mobility in simulated combat. Similarly, when he was chief of the Army Concept Team in Vietnam in 1963, testing the helicopter gunship's merit in a real war, his superior "officer" was the secretary of the Army, who had assigned him there; and not the Joint Chiefs of Staff who, for varying reasons, opposed the whole exercise.

Each time Rowny was given one of these high-visibility jobs, experimenting with helicopters, he suffered another storm of threats and insults. Even more frequent were the times when Rowny encountered tough resistance while trying to obtain the equipment, housing, people, or whatever else he needed to run his program. One bright exception, to Rowny, was General Creighton Abrams. On the Army General Staff in the early 1960s, "Abrams," said Rowny "was our guardian angel." Abrams, too, was opposed to the investment in helicopters at the expense of tanks. But he told Rowny's self-appointed adversaries, very bluntly, "Out of fairness and decency, give him a chance to do the mission we sent him to do."

Rowny first "nestled up to helicopters," as he puts it, in Korea, fighting in 1951–52 alongside the Marine Corps. "They were using Air MEDEVAC [evacuation of wounded by helicopter]," he noted. "It completely reversed a statistic. Before Korea, 90% of all people with head or body wounds died. In Korea, and again in Vietnam, 90% of them lived." Helicopters also were first used there for pin-point attack on enemy guerrilla units. Between 1952 and 1955, while a principal member of the Infantry School faculty, Rowny titled that tactic "The Swarm of Bees." First, its plan said, stun the enemy with a thunderous bombardment; then, before he can recover from the shock, send troops in helicopter gunships swarming onto the target.

Much of this is "old hat" now. Briefly summarized, says Rowny, "In the Vietnam War, our tests proved beyond a doubt that the use of armed helicopters in counterinsurgency, in precision attack without a lot of collateral damage to civilian populations, was here to stay." Indeed, Air MEDEVAC and the use of the helicopter in police patrols are common practices today in most large American cities.

As with the helicopter business, Rowny's career in arms-reduction diplomacy often pushed him in directions he didn't' want to go. From 1971 to 1973, Rowny was deputy chairman of NATO's Military Committee, NATO's counterpart, roughly, to the U.S. Joint Chiefs of Staff. Very early, the committee chairman, German general Johannes Steinhoff, appointed Rowny chairman of a Mutual Balanced Force Reductions (MBFR) planning group.

He had two reasons for picking Rowny: (1) he wanted NATO to initiate talks with the Soviets over reduction of conventional arms in Europe; and (2) he particularly wanted an American involved because the United States, at the time, was more interested, for several reasons, in strategic arms and human rights negotiations. Rowny had spent almost two years organizing the NATO proposals for MBFR when, in 1973, he was pressured to serve, and did until mid-1979, as Joint Chiefs of Staff representative to, and their principal advisor on, SALT II (the second edition of Strategic Arms Limitation Talks).

It was a job he didn't want in 1973 because he thought MBFR much more important, and, in 1976, he tried to leave for a lucrative offer in private industry. Both times, "My good friend [U.S. Senator Henry M.] 'Scoop' Jackson gave me his 'Duty, Honor, Country' speech; and the second time, my West Point classmate, [Joint Chiefs Chairman] George Brown, said simply, 'I need you.' What could I do?"

Still, says General Andrew P. O'Meara, a friend who was Rowny's Army boss for a time, "As it turned out, he had a much greater influence over national security policy—and he stayed in the decision-making arena a great deal longer—doing what he ended up doing, than he would have if he'd stayed in the Army after 1979." On the other hand, notes Colonel Sam Watson, who was Rowny's executive assistant for several of those negotiating years, "There was always somebody around who wanted to fire Rowny."

Military Leaders Since World War II

Pope John Paul II greets Rowny at the Vatican.
(From the collection of Edward Rowny)

Rowny resigned first, in June 1979, telling the Joint Chiefs chairman and the secretary of state he could not live with their lop-sided SALT II deal, which granted strategic weapons superiority to the Soviets. Said Kirk Lewis, Rowny's State Department aide, in 1988–90, "Now, you know *nobody* resigns over an *arms treaty* for heavens sake. But Rowny did because he felt SALT II was bad for the country."

In September 1979, testifying to the Senate Foreign Affairs Committee, Rowny's performance, says Lewis, "was classic 'Ed Rowny': well prepared, concise in his presentation; yet, not a lost thought nor inappropriate word." Rowny's testimony was the main reason the Senate denied the White House the 66 favorable votes needed to ratify the treaty.

In the end, Rowny had worked for four presidents and logged more than 2,000 hours negotiating with the Soviets. Other than eliminating an entire class of intermediate-range nuclear weapons, he says today, "Arms treaties haven't done anything to stop the growth of Soviet arms." Even his long-sought MBFR, now the

52

Conventional Forces Reduction in Europe (CFRE) treaty, was violated by the Soviets after it was initialed in late 1990. His frustration may have surfaced after he retired in June 1990. Did he prefer to be called, he was asked, general or ambassador? Rowny answered, "It took me 20 years to make General; it took only about 20 minutes to make me an ambassador. Call me General."

Possibly the best assessment of Rowny's career came from General Andrew Goodpaster, whose own career path crossed Rowny's several times. "He obviously knew how to command in combat," said Goodpaster. "His decorations prove that. But, what impressed me most was Rowny's being capable of precise, independent thought; and his moral courage to take a stand."

Chronology

April 3, 1917	Edward Leon Rowny born in Baltimore, Maryland
1937	graduates from Johns Hopkins University
1941	graduates from the U.S. Military Academy
1942–1945	serves, mostly with combat-engineer units, during World War II battles in North Africa and Italy
1949	graduates from Yale University with master's degrees in engineering and in international relations
1949-1952	serves with the U.S. Army Far East Command, mostly in combat planning and command during the Korean War
1959	graduates from the National War College
1961	promoted to brigadier general and made chief, Army Concept Team, Vietnam; promoted to major general in 1962

1965	becomes commander, 24th Infantry Division, in Germany; then deputy chief of staff, logistics, for U.S. Army Europe
1969	becomes U.S. Army deputy chief of staff for research and development
1970	promoted to lieutenant general
1971	becomes deputy chairman of the North Atlantic Treaty Organization's Military Committee
1973	serves as Joint Chiefs of Staff representative to the SALT II (Strategic Arms Limitation Talks) until his resignation from the Army in 1979
1981	returns to government service as ambassador, head of the U.S. team in Strategic Arms Reduction Talks (START) with the Soviets
1985	becomes special advisor to the president and the secretary of state on arms control matters until his retirement in June 1990. He now resides in Arlington, Virginia

Decorations: in addition to unit citations, campaign ribbons and foreign-government medals, his personal awards include the DSM, 3SS, 4LM, BSM for valor, AM, 2CR, 2CIB.

Further Reading

By Edward Rowny
 "Arms Control at Arm's Length," *Proceedings*, May 1990, p. 54 (publication of the U.S. Naval Institute, Annapolis, MD 21402).

Rowny, Lt. Gen. Edward L. "How *Not* to Negotiate With the Russians," *The Readers Digest*, June 1981, p. 66.

"Required for Arms Control," *The Washington Times*, September 18, 1989, p. F-1.

"10 'Commandments' for Negotiating With the Soviet Union," *The New York Times*, January 12, 1986.

Official Papers

Bureau of Public Affairs. *Current Policy No. 1088*: "Negotiating with the Soviet Union: Then and Now," U.S. Department of State, Washington, D.C. 20520.

Bureau of Public Affairs. *Current Policy No. 1112*: "East-West Relations and Arms Reductions," U.S. Department of State, Washington, D.C. 20520.

Office of History, Office of the Chief of Engineers. *Oral History: Rowny, Ambassador (Lt.G) Edward L. (USA Rtd)*; *Engineer Memoirs*, Washington, D.C., 1991. (Contact: Reference Branch; U.S. Army Military History Institute; Carlisle Barracks, PA 17013-5008—or libraries with telephone access to microfiche networks can view "Oral History" on their PC screens.)

Admiral Arleigh A. Burke

One of Burke's favorite photographs of himself.
(U.S. Naval Historical Center photograph, courtesy of
Admiral A. A. Burke, 1977)

Another Chief of Naval Operations (CNO), Admiral Thomas H. Moorer, was asked once for his opinion of his former boss, Admiral Arleigh Burke. "Well, of course, I can't say enough good about Arleigh Burke. He's the salt of the Earth. I don't think anybody in this century has made the impact on the Navy that he has."

Certainly, no other American naval officer in this century has so many things named in his honor: an entire group, the Burke Class, of guided-missile destroyers; an Arleigh A. Burke Hall at the

Admiral Arleigh A. Burke

Naval War College in Newport, Rhode Island; an Arleigh A. Burke Chair at the Center for Strategic and International Studies; an annual Arleigh A. Burke Competition for the best essay in leadership at the Naval Academy.

Ironically, while Arleigh Burke was growing up near Boulder, Colorado, the U.S. Navy didn't figure in his plans at all. His Swedish grandfather, Anders Bjorkgren, had come to America in 1857, and renamed himself "August Burke" to eliminate the difficulty people had with his real name. He ended up in Colorado; staked out a homestead there; and opened the first bakery in the pioneer town of Denver. August Burke's second oldest child, Oscar, was both a cowboy and a goldminer before he, too, claimed a homestead five miles east of Boulder and married a Boulder schoolteacher, Clara Mokler.

Arleigh (a name his mother invented) Albert Burke was born of that marriage, the first of six children (four daughters and two sons), in 1901. Burke's elementary school was a one-room schoolhouse built on land donated by his father. The schoolteachers, who usually roomed at Burke's home, "had to know their stuff," says Burke, "or they didn't get hired; they had to be able to enforce discipline or they'd have chaos; and they had to be dedicated because they taught all eight grades," a total of about 30 students from one year to the next.

On the other hand, he says, "Kids didn't go to school then, if they didn't want to." By the time they were 13 or so, they could, and were needed to, do an adult's work on their family farms. But Arleigh's mother wanted him to earn a high school diploma, and hopefully then a college degree. And Arleigh favored that plan, in part because meeting deadlines for getting his assigned farm chores done, "was a drudge." His father didn't care too much for the plan, he says, "Until my mother volunteered to do my chores while I was in high school—and she was as good as any man at most things on the farm."

Being a student was no easier for Burke, however, than being a teenage cowboy might have been. For one thing, the agreement was that Arleigh could attend high school only so long as his class grades were superior. Every time they sagged a little, his mother, or one of the resident gradeschool teachers, hammered extra instruction into him on nights and weekends. In addition, the closest high school—actually a preparatory school for college—was in Boulder, a 10-mile round trip on horseback every school day.

Military Leaders Since World War II

However, looking back decades later, Burke said being born into a country-school competition, "was the greatest thing that ever happened to me. That whole experience taught me to work. And to enjoy it." Still, his parents couldn't afford to send him to Colorado State College, now the University of Colorado. So, they urged him to try to qualify for the U.S. Military Academy. When he applied there, however, he learned the roster for 1919 had been filled. West Point suggested he try Annapolis.

In spite of standout grades in high school plus the help of three months' study in Missouri at a Naval Academy testing-preparation school, Burke barely passed the entrance tests. When he entered the Naval Academy in June 1919, the 17-year-old Plebe was on the defensive. "I felt far less prepared than the other boys," he says. "I had to work like hell," and, he decided years later, "I just never got over the habit." He graduated in 1923, ranked 71st in a class of 413.

Ensign Burke's first assignment was to the battleship *Arizona* on the West Coast from 1923 to 1928.[1] In 1926, he earned a promotion to lieutenant, junior grade. He also learned all about the ship, where she might leak, what strains she could handle when underway, "all her little peculiarities." After the *Arizona*, he spent a year on the supply ship *Procyon*. He received a commendation letter for the, "rescue of ship-wrecked and sea-faring men" during that tour. Burke's next 10 years in the Navy were spent partly as a gunnery officer or navigator on a destroyer but mostly going to school. He took postgraduate instruction in ordnance and military supply; and spent a year at the University of Michigan, earning a master's degree in chemical engineering.

Basically, Burke was doing a lot of highly technical work, the kind of thing not noticed much outside his field. He was not discouraged, however, even though, promoted to lieutenant in 1930, he had to wait eight more years for promotion to lieutenant commander. "A person's prospects in the Navy are very good," he says today. "Always have been. Not because it's the Navy, but because of the conditions of the world. We will always have to have a Navy to protect our commercial ships, our very long sea coasts, United States outposts overseas."

The one thing an officer needs to guard against, he quickly adds, is ego. "The very worst thing that happens in the Navy is when someone starts fiddling with professional affairs in order to push

---

[1]Sunk in the Japanese attack on Hawaii, December 7, 1941, the *Arizona* is now a war memorial in Pearl Harbor.

Admiral Arleigh A. Burke

their own personal advancement. That's fatal. They nearly always bitch it up. You have to commit yourself simply to learning to be a good general officer. That's the strength of the military in the United States."

Lt. Commander Burke began to edge toward Navy center-stage in 1939 when he received his first command, of the destroyer USS *Mugford*. At the end of that one-year tour, in a short-range gunnery competition, all four of his ship's guns scored 100% hits on their targets, which is like hitting home runs all five at-bats in a baseball game. The *Mugford* won that year's Destroyer Gunnery Trophy; and, for a while, Burke was known as "King of the Cans" (Navy slang for destroyers).

In July 1940, Burke was reassigned to the Naval Gun Factory in Washington, D.C., as an inspector. Basically, that job meant supervising the purchase, test and delivery of munitions to the Navy's combat ships and submarines. For nearly a year after the Japanese attacked Pearl Harbor, Burke persistently requested transfer to combat duty. His main problem was his gun factory commander thought him invaluable right where he was.

Being a relentless pest did finally pay off, however. In January 1943, six months after his promotion to commander, he was shipped to the Pacific. During the next 14 months, he commanded four different destroyer squadrons. The most famous was the last, Destroyer Division 23, a squadron of nine ships. When he took command in October, he promptly christened ships and crews, "The Little Beavers." Between November 1943 and February 1944, Burke's Little Beavers sank 12 Japanese combatant ships, two support vessels, four barges, and shot down about 30 enemy aircraft—all without losing one Little Beaver.

Their "speed and daring," said the citations, earned Burke and his crews a flock of combat medals. A principal reason was that Burke ignored most of the official instructions, and rewrote Navy doctrine for destroyer tactics at sea. He also acquired a new nickname, "31-knot Burke." (A knot equals 1 nautical mile per hour or about 1.15 miles per hour on land.) War correspondents assumed, and so reported to America, that "31-knot Burke" was driving his ships into battle at top speed. Actually, he wanted his ships overhauled so they could deliver sustained speeds of about 34–35 knots. His request to do that was denied. Burke resorted to the needle. When his boss, Admiral William F. "Bull" Halsey, in Hawaii wired him once to redeploy his ships "quickly," to a new

Military Leaders Since World War II

Vice Admiral Marc Mitscher and his chief of staff on the flag bridge of the carrier USS Randolph, *off Okinawa, in June 1945.*
(U.S. Naval Historical Center photograph)

---

location, Burke wired back sarcastically, "Am proceeding at 31 knots." Halsey's reply began: "To 31-knot Burke."

Explains Burke about the serious side of all this: "To maintain maximum speed for a long time means having quality equipment, well-maintained, and well-trained, quality people." Obtaining those assets takes time and effort, he says, but they also mean winning battles of many kinds. "A fine rule to follow," he claims, "is to get going sooner than anticipated, travel faster than expected, and arrive before you're due. That's true in just about anything you do, diplomacy, engineering, business management, anything."

In March 1944, "31-knot Burke" was named chief of staff of the First Carrier Task Force, commanded by naval aviation pioneer Admiral Marc Mitscher. Burke hadn't wanted to leave his destroyers, and Mitscher didn't want a non-aviator for his chief of staff.

Admiral Arleigh A. Burke

The expert on naval aviation and the expert on surface warfare made a good team, however. By war's end, Mitscher was promoting Burke as a future Navy CNO.

After the war, one of Burke's most important assignments, as it turned out, was spending 16 months on the Navy General Board. There, he instigated a study, published in July 1948, on "National Security and Naval Contributions for the next 10 years." That subject led naturally to an assignment which almost ended Burke's naval career. The job title seemed innocuous enough: assistant chief of naval operations for organizational research and policy, in the Office of the Chief of Naval Operations. Its Navy code designation was OP-23. Burke headed it from December 1948 to November 1949. OP-23 was the focal point for what became known as "The Revolt of the Admirals."

Basically, claims Burke, "OP-23 was a defensive organization to start with. But you can't defend yourself unless you get into the other guy's camp and find out what he's doing." In this case, "The Air Force wanted a monopoly on the big [atomic] weapons; and, for the good of the Nation's security, you can't afford to let any service have a monopoly on anything."

But air power advocates, supported by President Truman's White House and Secretary of Defense Louis A. Johnson, disagreed, claiming the nation's first line of defense would be atomic bombs aboard Air Force strategic bombers. The centerpiece of the Navy's argument, drawn primarily from its general board study, was a "supercarrier" from which medium bombers, carrying atomic weapons, could launch and land. In 1949, when Johnson canceled Navy plans, already approved by Congress, to build a "supercarrier," the "Revolt of the Admirals" erupted.

Charge and counter-charge were hurled publicly between unnamed Navy and Air Force "spokesmen," denigrating each other's service. It was a sad period in military history, "close to treason at times," said one Pentagon historian, because a by-product of the cat-fight was U.S. military secrets being handed to the Soviets via U.S. newspaper headlines. OP-23 generally, and Burke specifically, were accused of instigating most of this "insubordination." Burke's name was struck from the promotion list for rear admiral. His spectacular war record may have saved him from worse penalties.

Admiral Forrest Sherman, then-Chief of Naval Operations, cajoled his name back onto the list in mid-1950. Ironically, Sherman also received permission from Congress that year to re-start "supercarrier" construction. Not until May 1952, however, did Burke receive his rear admiral's "flag," as the Navy calls it—with a notice that the official record would credit him with having held the rank since July 1950. By then, he already had finished another angry, though brief, clash with some of Washington's politico-diplomatic leaders.

While commander of Cruiser Division Five in the Far East, he was also (from September to December 1951) a member of the United Nations Military Armistice negotiation team in Korea under Admiral C. Turner Joy. General Matthew Ridgway had praised the team to a joint session of Congress as "drawn from the

Admiral Burke on the signal bridge of the Gyatt, *awaiting launch of a Terrier missile.*
(Official U.S. Navy photograph, Naval Photographic Center)

best the nation produces in character, intellect, competence, loyalty, devotion to duty . . ." Team member, Army Maj. General Henry Hodes, said of Burke, "He contributed as much as anyone on the team. He was always strong, and he understood—as not many people in the United States, or the world, understand—communist ways of attacking any subject. If I ever have to head up a delegation such as this one again, I would want Burke first."

For his part, Burke was convinced the U.S. State Department in Washington was undercutting its own team in Korea, accepting Communist demands "so clearly not in our country's interest." In frustration, Burke finally told Harry S. Truman, "Mr. President, General Ridgway is a wonderful man. He submits recommendations he feels are in the best interest of our country; but nobody pays any attention."

Long before the newly elected President Eisenhower broke that impasse (by threatening the Chinese Communists with an "all-out atomic war" he had absolutely no intention of really starting), Burke was back in the office of the Chief of Naval Operations as director of strategic plans (OP-30). Since OP-30 develops plans for using naval power under almost every conceivable threat, being director of it was, for Burke, a logical follow-on to his time on the general board and, later, as head of OP-23.

When he left OP-30 in March 1954, to command Cruiser Division Six for only nine months and then the Atlantic Fleet's Destroyer Force for only six more, the soothsayers began to predict, "Our next CNO." The noise rose to a din in June 1955, when Burke was jumped in rank from rear admiral to full admiral. And the forecast was confirmed in August 1955, when President Eisenhower also jumped him over 92 more senior officers to Chief of Naval Operations. He would serve in that slot an unprecedented three terms. Summed up Rear Admiral Henry L. Miller, "He was absolutely dedicated to the Navy. He never let up. He had tons of energy. He knew no hours. You never knew what assignment you were going to get next, day or night."

The Navy as it is today began to take shape largely as a result of decisions made during the six years he was that service's top officer. He shopped the supermarket of technology at least as well as any other military leader since World War II. To cite just a few of the results: submarine-launched ballistic missiles; nuclear-powered ships and submarines (though Rear Admiral Hyman Rickover takes most of the credit for the latter); world leadership in anti-submarine warfare; an unmatched air defense system for surface ships; cruise missiles; and as many communications and reconnaissance satellites as the Air Force uses.

A good deal of credit for this amazing performance Burke attributes to competition, both among contractors to the Navy and between the Navy and Army/Air Force. "Fear of duplication," he argues, "is a stupid damn fear. We get better cars, for instance, at lower prices because of competition. If there wasn't any competition between the Army, Navy and Air Force, you'd have to create it. There's always some lunkhead around who doesn't know something can't be done, so he does it."

In one sense, for Burke at least, that brings him back full circle to the hard work and education drilled into him from childhood. "There is no way a stupid individual can become a military leader," he says, "except by fraud. The hard fact is, you can't lead quality people well unless you're bright enough, dedicated enough and well-trained yourself." Maybe that's why, when he was CNO and someone requested an autographed picture, he always signed it, "A. Burke, sailor, 1st/c."

Chronology

October 19, 1901	Arleigh Albert Burke born in Boulder, Colorado
1923	graduates from the U.S. Naval Academy
1928	Ensign Burke completes five years' service, including promotion to lieutenant, junior grade, on the battleship USS *Arizona*
1931	Lieutenant Burke earns a master's degree in chemical engineering from the University of Michigan
1938	promoted to lieutenant commander and assigned command of the destroyer USS *Mugford*

Admiral Arleigh A. Burke

1940–1945 spends the first half of World War II as a naval gun factory inspector in Washington, D.C.; the last half commanding destroyer divisions in battle and, then, as chief of staff of the Navy's main aircraft carrier task force in the Pacific. Tour includes promotions to, first, commander and then captain

1951 while in command of Cruiser Division Five in the Pacific, participates in Korean War truce talks as a rear admiral

1954 leaves post as Navy director of strategic plans, in the Pentagon to take command of Cruiser Division Six

1955 becomes commander of the Atlantic Fleet's Destroyer Force with promotion to upper half of rear admiral ranks

August 17, 1955 to August 1, 1961 serves as Chief of Naval Operations, retires in 1961. After a few years as an industrial consultant, Burke was forced by failing eyesight to retire completely. He and his wife now live in a retirement home in Arlington, Virginia

Decorations: in addition to more than 40 unit citations, campaign ribbons, and foreign-government medals, his personal awards include the DSC, 3DSM, 4LM, SS, CR, PH.

Further Reading

By Arleigh Burke
"The Lebanon Crisis," *Proceedings, Naval History Symposium*, U.S. Naval Academy, Annapolis, Md., 1973.

"National Strategy," *Naval War College Review 19*, October 1965, pp. 21–35.

Contact, also, for several Burke "Oral Histories," the Oral History Department, U.S. Naval Institute, Annapolis, MD 21402.

About Arleigh Burke

Jones, Ken, and Hubert Kelley. *Admiral Arleigh (31-Knot) Burke: The Story of a Fighting Sailor*. Phila.: Chilton, 1962.

Love, Robert William, Jr., editor. *The Chiefs of Naval Operations*. Annapolis, Md: Naval Institute Press, 1980.

Potter, E. B. *Admiral Arleigh Burke: A Biography*. New York: Random House, 1990.

Rosenberg, David Allen. "Officer Development in the Interwar Navy: Arleigh Burke—The Making of a Naval Professional, 1919–1940," *Pacific Historical Review 44*, November 1975.

Wolfert, Ira. *The Battle of the Solomons*. Boston: Houghton Miflin, 1943; won a Pulitzer Prize.

Admiral Thomas H. Moorer

Moorer during a quiet moment in one of his offices.
(Official U.S. Navy photo, Department of Defense Still Media Records Center)

On the day in May 1955 when the U.S. Senate approved the nomination of Admiral Arleigh Burke to become Chief of Naval Operations, he was attending a briefing at the Norfolk, Virginia Naval Base on the nuclear-weapon capabilities of the Atlantic Fleet. The man giving the briefing was 43-year-old Navy Captain Thomas H. Moorer.

A dozen years later, Moorer also would become Chief of Naval Operations. Then, in July 1970, Moorer would be promoted to chairman of the Joint Chiefs of Staff, only the second Navy officer to be named Joint Chiefs chairman since that office was created in 1949. Unlike Burke, Moorer had taken "the aviation route," as the Navy puts it, to reach the top of first the Navy's and then the nation's military leadership. But, in many respects, the history of Moorer's teenage years reads like Burke's.

Military Leaders Since World War II

Thomas Hinman Moorer was born in 1912 in Mount Willing, Alabama, north of Montgomery. His father, Richard Randolph, was a dentist. His mother, Hulda Hinson Moorer, taught school until the first of her four children was born. "Then," writes one Moorer biographer, "she devoted her life to her family, church, and the preservation of historic records of the Confederacy." Claimed Tom Moorer in a nationally televised interview years later, "If everybody had had my mother and father, we wouldn't have any problems today; probably wouldn't even need any policemen."

Maxwell Field (now Maxwell Air Force Base) was located near Mt. Willing. Consequently, Moorer watched his first airplane flight when he was only six. It infected him with what became a career-long ailment, "the flying bug." Only eight families lived in Mt. Willing, so all seven elementary-school grades were taught in a one-room school-house. Moorer was one of just three students in his own class.

Says Moorer, "We had none of this stuff we have today of a teacher getting sued for spanking a child. Because she demanded we behave, she had no problem of unruly children disrupting class. I don't think kids in school today get very much of either one: tough discipline or learning."

Moorer finished the seventh grade at age 12. The family moved to Montgomery then and in June 1927 Moorer graduated from high school, valedictorian of his class, at age 15. (When only 14, he had 18 course credits, two more than the minimum required; and could have graduated then.) "Part of my training at home," he said, "was learning how important it was not to fail. I wasn't allowed to go out and play until my homework was done to my parents' satisfaction."

As Moorer graduated from high school, his father bought a dental practice in Eufaula, also near Montgomery. Because he calls Eufaula his hometown, Moorer has endowed a trust fund at Eufaula's Middle School. Each year, it awards cash prizes to the students who write the three best essays on the topic: What America Means to Me. "And those kids write damn good essays," he reports. "If we just stand by those youngsters, this country will be all right."

Moorer's strongest interest among his high school courses was on "the technical side," as he describes it, i.e. physics, chemistry, mathematics, etc., because, he says, "they always came easy to me for some reason." Thus, his college goal was Georgia Tech, one of the best engineering universities in the South; but the Great Depression of the 1930s fouled up that plan. With his savings gone due to a wave of bank failures, and with three other children to support, Richard Moorer announced that Georgia Tech would have to wait a while.

Admiral Thomas H. Moorer

Moorer then tried to enroll at West Point, to get his degree at taxpayer expense. Its entrance class for 1928 was full, however, so he shifted to the Naval Academy. Still, the best a local congressman could do in 1928 was to list Moorer as first alternate in 1929. Moorer passed the entrance examinations, but the congressman reneged on his promise. However, one of Alabama's U.S. senators then was persuaded to name Moorer his first alternate—aided in making that decision by Moorer's father, a power in Alabama politics at the time.

Very early at Annapolis, he was nicknamed "Dead Eye" because, on the rifle range, he consistently drilled the center of the target. Having that skill impressed him far less than it did his classmates. "In Mt. Willing," he said, "there was nothing much to do on weekends except go hunting. I'd been shooting for 10 years. Most of the guys" in his Naval Academy class "had never held a rifle before." The six-foot, 195-pound Moorer also played varsity football for three years.

Moorer's consuming interest, however, was in his studies—except for his mandatory course in Spanish. "I almost ran aground over that one," he says. But the rest of the curriculum was pushing state-of-the-art technology, in general, and aviation technology, specifically. Years later, he would claim, "If a Naval officer doesn't have much interest in engineering, much curiosity about the outer reaches of technology, he's probably not going to be a very effective Naval officer. In war or peace, the Navy is a 'technical' service."

As June graduation approached for Moorer's Class of 1933, the Depression tossed more obstacles in front of him. For one, Congress decreed only the top half of the 432 graduates would receive an ensign's commission. Those midshipmen whose test scores, their senior year, ranked them lower than that would graduate with a college engineering degree, but no commission—in other words, no job.

In addition, newly commissioned ensigns had to agree: (a) to a 15% pay cut; (b) to a delay of two years before they could enter the higher-paying naval aviation field; and (c) to promise not to get married for two years after graduation. "Try that, today," says Moorer, "and somebody probably would sue you, claiming a violation of their civil rights. We just accepted it then as necessary and reasonable under the circumstances."

And, he still thinks "the marriage thing" was a good idea. "My class has the lowest divorce rate of any class at the Academy. With most classes, you've been confined and chaperoned so long, you're ready to grab the first skirt that comes along. We were forced to think about who we'd like to marry for life."

Military Leaders Since World War II

Moorer studied hard that last semester; and, in spite of football and other distractions, managed to graduate just under the wire, ranked 174th in his class. In another effort to cut its payroll, the Navy ordered the 216 survivors, all ensigns now, to take another set of tests. The best scores this time would be kept on the payroll; the others likely dismissed. Moorer's test results ranked him 80th among the 216.

Abiding by the two-year-wait rule, Moorer entered flight training as soon as he was allowed, in 1935. A year later, he had his wings. "In those days," he says, "you had to fly everything, seaplanes, bombers, fighters, reconnaissance aircraft. We weren't being trained to be pilots, but to be commanders of squadrons and air wings. So we had to learn what all the aircraft could do." He served in fighter squadrons from 1936 to 1939, and with patrol squadrons for the next three years.

His 12 patrol aircraft were in Hawaii when the Japanese attacked Pearl Harbor. On December 8, 1941, he received from Washington what he believes was the classic dumb order of World War II: "Be prepared to take your six or 12 planes East or West." Ten of his planes had been destroyed in the Japanese attack.

Until June 1942, he flew reconnaissance, rescue, and re-supply missions, mostly around the Dutch East Indies (Indonesia today). Evidence enough of how often he flew in harm's way, is that, during that short time, he earned a Silver Star, Distinguished Flying Cross, and Purple Heart; a patrol squadron he commanded received a Presidential Unit Citation "for extraordinary heroism."

Immediately after the war, Moorer received what he still thinks was the most interesting assignment of his career. He was sent to Japan for 10 months with a Strategic Bombing Survey team. "We asked a million questions," he says. The team also found, in a cave, a library containing copies of every message between Japan's high command and its land and sea forces fighting the war. What amazed Moorer most, from that library, was learning that the Japanese game plan, in starting its Asian war, wasn't at all what the United States had thought it was in 1941.

The Japanese objective was to seize the raw wealth of, principally, oil, rubber, tin, and rice, in Southeast Asia and Indonesia to feed its own growing population and industrial base at home. Further, its attack on Pearl Harbor was designed solely to cripple the Navy's Pacific Fleet so it could not interfere with that Japanese, mostly sea-transported, invasion plan.

Admiral Thomas H. Moorer

When it had conquered what it wanted, Japan planned to offer to give back the Philippines as an incentive to the United States to accept an armistice. Japan's strategy counted a great deal on its conviction that Americans would have no stomach for war. Among the events of 1940–41 that led Japan to this conclusion were: Congress enacting a draft law by only one vote; America reelecting President Franklin D. Roosevelt, overwhelmingly, on his promise "to keep our boys out of war"; the U.S. Army training with rifles carved from tree limbs and tanks made of plywood.

Evidently, only Admiral Isoroku Yamamoto, who had planned and led the Pearl Harbor assault, had strong doubts about the success of this Japanese strategy. One of the very few Japanese leaders who had spent several years in the United States, Yamamoto said quietly, as the rest of Japan rejoiced over their Pearl Harbor victory, "I fear all we have managed to do is awaken a sleeping giant, and fill him with a terrible wrath."

For Moorer, all this was just real-world confirmation of certain principles, basic, he believes, to both combat readiness and providing for the national security. One of those, he says, is, "It's not what you've got that's important. What's important is what the other guy thinks you're willing to do with what you've got."

In addition, he argues, "The Navy, because it's mobile, can change its strategies all the time, adapt to changing situations. I never have believed in a single strategy, a single weapon system. Unless you know when you're going to war and who you're going to fight, you can't make that kind of decision. You have to be prepared as much as you can for any eventuality."

During the 15 years prior to his becoming Chief of Naval Operations (CNO) in 1967, he helped develop new Navy ordnance; aided CNO Arleigh Burke in strategic planning; served with cruiser divisions and carrier task forces. Then, between 1962 and 1967, he commanded first, the Seventh Fleet; then the Pacific Fleet; and, finally, the Atlantic Fleet.[1] With that unprecedented set of top commands on his record, the rest of the Navy was not surprised at all when he was nominated to be CNO.

---

[1] Moorer was both promoted to admiral and assigned command of the Pacific Fleet in June 1964. After Congress passed the Gulf of Tonkin Resolution that August, Moorer flew to Washington to argue, face-to-face, for permission to blockade North Vietnam's Haiphong Harbor. "That would end the war very quickly," he argued, "because 95% of Hanoi's war-fighting material is coming from Russia into North Vietnam through that port." His request was denied.

Claimed Admiral David L. McDonald, who preceded Moorer as CNO, "Probably no other man has entered the office of Chief of Naval Operations so well prepared by previous background and assignments as has Admiral Moorer." Added a leader of the Senate Armed Services Committee, Senator John Tower, "Moorer is one of the finest military professionals our nation ever has produced."

Moorer's tour as CNO occurred while U.S. combat in Southeast Asia was the fiercest, involving the largest numbers of U.S. forces. At the same time, beginning in 1967, public objection to the war began to climb. Consequently, both President Lyndon Johnson and Congress deemed it political suicide to increase taxes in order to pay the war's increased costs. Thus, the Pentagon had to shift resources from Europe, Japan, and elsewhere to Vietnam, in effect paying about 20% of the war's annual cost out of inventory, so to speak.

That was doubly difficult for the Navy because, at the same time the Vietnam War peaked, the Soviets began moving large naval task forces into the Mediterranean, the Red Sea, and the Indian Ocean. (By 1970, the Soviet Pacific Fleet alone was larger than the number of surface combatant ships in the entire U.S. Navy worldwide.)

Sums up a book by the Joint Chiefs' Historical Division, "Despite fiscal constraints and the needs of the Vietnam war ... Moorer marshaled available resources to counter the [Soviet] expansion. [He] was particularly successful in modernizing U.S. submarines with the latest technology to assure their continued supremacy"—an interesting piece of praise since Moorer's first love, personally, was naval aviation.

In July 1970, Moorer succeeded Army General Earle Wheeler as chairman of the Joint Chiefs of Staff; and the national security issues he faced ballooned in size and significance. Noted former Vice Admiral John T. Hayward, a kindred soul to Moorer in many respects, "Tom Moorer was CNO and Joint Chiefs Chairman at a very difficult time."

For instance, he and the Joint Chiefs (including Generals Abrams and Brown) resisted orders from the secretary of defense and the president to withdraw all U.S. combat forces from Vietnam, and turn the fighting over to the South Vietnamese. They did not oppose the concept of "Vietnamization," as it was called. They simply thought the withdrawal rate was too fast. Moorer and the Chiefs lost that one. From a total of nearly 415,000 U.S. troops in Vietnam in 1970, the number had dropped to 25,000 by the end of 1972.

Admiral Thomas H. Moorer

On the other hand, in the spring of 1972, the South Vietnamese showed they were better trained by their U.S. advisers than the Joint Chiefs apparently thought they were. During what was called the "Easter-tide Offensive," an attacking force of some 500,000 North Vietnamese regulars was crushed by the South Vietnamese Army, Marine Corps, and Air Forces.

Encouraged by the South Vietnamese performance and determined to move peace talks in Paris off dead center, President Richard Nixon finally granted Moorer and the Joint Chiefs something they had been requesting for seven years: permission to mine the approaches to Haiphong Harbor and bombard previously prohibited targets elsewhere in North Vietnam. Under that pressure, the North Vietnamese caved in, at least briefly. In January 1973, they agreed, in a pact signed in Paris, to stop fighting. Immediately afterward, Moorer was ordered to disband MACV and bring home the remaining U.S. forces. The Vietnam War was officially ended for the United States.

Moorer succeeded in one other major crisis that erupted while he was chairman. In October 1973, Egypt and Syria

CNO Moorer being met on the flight deck of the Oriskany *by the carrier's commanding officer, Captain Jack S. Kenyon.*
(National Archives)

attacked Israeli forces stationed along the Golan Heights and the northern Sinai Peninsula, territory Israel had won from them during the Six Day War of 1967. Moorer endorsed an order already issued that weekend by Joint Chiefs member Air Force General George Brown. Brown had ordered, immediately, a major airlift to replace the heavy losses of equipment the Israeli's had suffered at the war's outset.

However, Moorer also feared that the Arabs would seek off-setting aid from the Soviet Union. And, indeed, when Israel began to sweep across the Red Sea into Egypt, the Soviets did threaten to intervene. Reports a file in the Joint Chiefs' History Division, "At a midnight meeting in the White House, Moorer said bluntly that the Middle East would be the worst place in the world to fight a war with the Soviet Union." As a result, though a worldwide military alert was ordered, to discourage Soviet aggression, U.S. pressure stopped Israel's advance and diplomatic work was begun to restore peace.

On most other basic issues Moorer's track record was the same as that of all other post–World War II military leaders. The soundness of his counsel did not become clear until well after he retired. For example, he argued during his entire chairmanship that U.S. conventional forces had been seriously weakened by a combination of the Vietnam War and inadequate military spending since. But, not until 1981 did a new president, Ronald Reagan, reverse the 1970s "decade of neglect," as Reagan called it, with sharply increased military budgets.

Similarly, all the Joint Chiefs opposed the provisions in the first Strategic Arms Limitation Treaty (SALT I) and its companion ABM (Anti-Ballistic Missile) pact. In a nutshell, they said the first would grant the Soviets a numerical advantage in strategic offensive weapons and the second would limit too greatly U.S. ability to build defenses against those Soviet weapons—and besides the Soviets, with impunity, could violate the provisions of both, anyway. All those Joint Chiefs predictions have since come true.

After he retired, Moorer often growled in interviews about "'anti-militarism,' which I look on more as 'anti-common sense'; the tendency by some—in and out of government—to devalue our defense requirements by studying the range of possible enemy *intentions*, rather than the *capabilities* of an unpredictable adversary. We must never forget," he once advised, "that, in international gamesmanship, there is no prize for second place. If we do not provide for the security of our country, all the country's other problems become moot."

America's next generation, he believes, is the key to a strong national defense. As he once told Naval Academy midshipmen, "As you climb the ladder of rank, authority and success, maintain contact with the young people. We're not smarter than they are; just older."

Chronology

February 9, 1912	Thomas Hinman Moorer born in Mt. Willing, Alabama
1933	graduates from the U.S. Naval Academy
1936	completes flight training at the U.S. Naval Air Station, Pensacola, and is promoted to lieutenant, junior grade
1941–1945	leads patrol aircraft squadrons in the South Pacific during the first half of the war, earning the Silver Star, Distinguished Flying Cross and Purple Heart; spends the last years of the war doing staff work and in command of flight- training missions for the Atlantic Fleet; is a commander by the end of the war
1952	promoted to captain while in charge of research and development testing at the Naval Ordnance Test Station, Inyokern, California
1958	promoted to rear admiral while working for the Chief of Naval Operations (CNO) in the Pentagon
1962	with designation as a vice admiral, takes command of the Seventh Fleet

1964	with promotion to admiral, takes command of the U.S. Pacific Fleet
1965	assigned as U.S. Atlantic Fleet Commander in Chief (CINC), and, concurrently, Supreme Allied Commander, Atlantic
1667	becomes Chief of Naval Operations (CNO)
1970	sworn in as chairman of the Joint Chiefs of Staff, he serves there until his retirement on July 1, 1974. Since then, while serving on several company boards of directors, among other things, he lists his official residence as Eufaula, Alabama, but also lives in McLean, Virginia, a Washington, D.C. suburb

Decorations: among more than 40 unit citations, campaign ribbons, foreign-government awards, his personal medals include 5DSM, SS, LM, DFC, PH.

Further Reading

By Thomas Moorer

Co-author with Alvin Cottrell. *U.S. Overseas Bases: Problems of Projecting American Military Power Abroad*. Beverly Hills: Sage Press, 1977.

"Global Evolution since World War II," in *Ideas, Their Origins, and Their Consequences*. Washington, D.C.: American Enterprise Institute for Public Policy Research, 1988.

About Thomas Moorer

"Armed Forces Change of Command," *Time*, July 6, 1970.

Admiral Thomas H. Moorer

Horrocks, Capt. John N., Jr. "The Art, Science, and Innocence in Becoming Chief of Naval Operations," *U.S. Naval Institute Proceedings*, January 1970, p. 18.

Love, Robert William, Jr., editor. *The Chiefs of Naval Operations*. Annapolis, Md.: Naval Institute Press, 1980.

Webb, Willard J. and Ronald H. Cole. *The Chairman of the Joint Chiefs of Staff*. Washington, D.C.: Historical Division, Joint Chiefs of Staff, 1989.

Vice Admiral John T. Hayward

Vice Admiral John T. "Chick" Hayward.
(Official U.S. Navy Photograph, Naval Photographic Center)

---

*V*ice Admiral John Tucker Hayward had been president of the Naval War College in Newport, Rhode Island for nearly three years when he retired on September 1, 1968. During his 43-year Navy career, he earned doctorates in nuclear physics and in law. He had logged more than 13,000 pilot hours, by far the most of any flag officer, and had made 300 aircraft-carrier landings. And, as he left the college, he drove past the more than $28 million worth of new facilities, built with funds he had finessed

Vice Admiral John T. Hayward

out of a reluctant Navy, White House, and Congress.[1] "Not too bad," said an old fan of his, "for a high school drop-out."

Hayward was born in New York in November 1908, the second son of Charles Brian and Rosa Valdetarro Hayward. His father was an automotive, radio, and aviation engineer—all brand-new technical fields then, in an age when most engineers, like most doctors, were general practitioners. Charles Hayward built a complete radio station in the attic of the family home in Great Neck, Long Island, and also worked with the Wright brothers, from time to time, helping them build their airplanes.

"He was very talented," says Hayward, "worked all the time." A prized possession in Admiral Hayward's library today is a copy of *Practical Aeronautics* by C. B. Hayward, published in 1912. "It's a sort-of 'How to build an airplane in your garage' book," says Hayward. The book's complimentary introduction was written by Orville Wright. Hayward loved boats as a boy. That affection may have been partly the result of his father, an outspoken advocate of the Navy from having served with it in the Spanish-American War. But that love of boats was overwhelmed by Hayward's teenage obsession with airplanes.

Hazelhurst Flying Field was near Great Neck. Consequently, early into Jack Hayward's grade school education, he'd already seen dirigibles over Hazelhurst and taken his first airplane ride, in a Jenny. He also believed going to school did not figure in the equation for learning to fly airplanes. Thus, in spite of the Jesuit discipline imposed at the Loyola School, where he was sent, he says his best subjects at the time were "day-dreaming" and "absent." His mother tried to encourage him to study by bringing home lots of books, but, he noted, "I really just didn't like school."

When he reached high school age, the tough discipline of Loyola was replaced by the equally tough discipline of Long Island's Oakdale Military Academy. That made no difference to Hayward. The academy finally expelled him, actually just recognizing he wasn't there much, anyway. He fled to Manhattan to live with his grandmother, and never went back. She got him a job as bat boy for the New York Yankees, a happy excuse for not

---

[1] The War College was established in a converted "poor house" in Newport, R.I. in 1884. From then until Hayward became its president in 1966, according to one budget report, the Navy had spent a total of only $894,000 on War College construction.

being in school. (He met such teenage idols as cowboy movie star Tom Mix, boxing champion Jack Dempsey, and, of course, baseball immortals such as Babe Ruth and Lou Gehrig.)

He was there when he learned about an alternate route he could take to a pilot's license, one that did not require the high school diploma he lacked. In 1923, Congress enacted a law that allowed a limited number of Navy enlisted men to take the Naval Academy's entrance tests. And, Hayward knew, Naval Academy graduates could be assigned to flight training. In May 1925, he enlisted. The recruiting officer didn't question his lie about being

"Chick" in World War II in the Pacific checks the painting job on his patrol bomber.
(U.S. Navy photograph, courtesy Vice Admiral J. T. Hayward, USN, ret.)

16, the minimum qualified age, and on June 29 at age 15, he reported to the Navy boot camp in Newport.

His drill instructor, a salty old bosun's mate, glared at the 110-pound Hayward in his first roll call, and growled, "How'd a young chicken like you get in here amongst all these grown men?" (By nightfall that day, he was, and would remain, "Chick" Hayward of the Navy.) Hayward soon hated the Navy as much as he had hated school. "It was greens and prunes for breakfast," he said, "drill, tie knots, and do housework all day long." He implored his father to confirm he was under age, and bail him out. But, says Hayward with some pride today, "My father was a very tough Englishman. He believed, when you made a decision, you should have to live with it."

Hayward's first sea duty was more of the same, merely adding to his growing fear that he was not on a route into aviation. Finally, he pleaded his ambition and his liabilities to ship's Chaplain John J. Brady. Commander Brady had been with the Marine Corps in Belleau Wood at the start of the Allies' savage drive to victory in World War I and he was as tough as any combat veteran. "He didn't mind at all hauling off and belting you one to get your attention," says Hayward. "He's the one who lowered the boom on me to study for the Academy entrance exams. He wouldn't even let me go ashore on weekends. 'Newport's too dangerous,' he'd say. 'There are *girls* out there!'"

Hayward devoted nine months to preparing for the tests, under constant pressure from Father Brady and, at the end, a Naval Academy preparatory school. Still, he said, "I had a terrible time passing just because I hadn't really ever been to school before." He did well in physics, geometry, and algebra; was good enough at American and English history; but barely passed English. He did pass, however, along with 18 other of the more than 100 enlisted men who took that year's exams, and, on July 13, 1926, he became a Naval Academy midshipman.

Hayward had won a much larger prize than that, however. The textbooks he once scorned had become assets, keys to solving all kinds of problems. Four years later, the high school drop-out graduated with scholastic honors, standing 58th in a class of 402. (He also was elected national All-American in water polo in 1930 after three years as a member of Navy's intercollegiate championship team.)

He then volunteered for the pre-flight test at Hampton Roads, Virginia, a preliminary to flight training at Pensacola, Florida. The test amounted to 15 flying hours in a one-float, ocher-colored seaplane so unstable even experienced pilots called it "The Yellow Peril." The test objective was simply to find out which volunteers might have enough natural talent to become good pilots. Hayward soloed after seven hours of instruction.

He was one of only 67 out of the 134 volunteers sent to Hampton Roads who were certified for Pensacola. While awaiting his transfer, he was ordered to temporary duty on a light cruiser. It, in turn, soon sailed to Central America to protect Americans suddenly caught in the crossfire of a Honduran civil war. The Coast Guard, an agency of the U.S. Treasury in peacetime, awarded Hayward a Silver Life Saving Medal while he was there, for saving the lives of a swimming party off Tela, Honduras. But his "temporary duty" delayed for a year, until late 1931, his arrival at Pensacola's Naval Air Station.

"Pensacola then," says Hayward, "was the father and mother-in-law of naval aviation." Part of its year-long training program was classroom study of an aircraft's three basic elements: engine, airframe, and electronics/communications. The other half was, depending on the weather, up to 300 hours of flight time in every kind of aircraft the Navy owned. And, each time his instructor gave a student a down-check on a particular flying lesson, the student had to fly that same lesson for two other instructors. "If one of them also gave you a down-check," says Hayward, "you were in real trouble." Almost predictably, of the 67 students who began flight training, only Hayward and 16 others were awarded their wings in October 1932.

By the mid-1930s, however, Hayward was shopping for another way to earn a living. He was driven to it by the Navy's small size, only 3,500 officers at the time. Moreover, on the list, competing for a rarely offered promotion, were a very large number of junior officers with twice Hayward's six years time-in-grade. As proof to him of his dismal forecast, he was told to take another test, in 1932, if he wished to become a lieutenant, junior grade. Then he was told, even if he passed, he would remain an ensign—with an 8 percent cut in pay.

Hayward did see a promising career option. "It seemed to me," he decided, "that knowing physics, nuclear physics," an obscure engineering discipline then, "should make me valuable to somebody in commercial industry." But, the bleak economy of 1932 told Hayward, newly married and planning a family by then, not to rush into a career change. So, from 1932 to 1937, he flew with

Vice Admiral John T. Hayward

Navy scouting and patrol squadrons, usually as commander, and fattened his flight log constantly with extra duty. He saw nearly all of South America that way, on one tour. On another, he picked up six extra dollars a day, a healthy amount back then, ferrying aircraft back and forth across the United States.

Then, from mid-1937 through September 1942, three different assignments—the first two as aviator on two different cruisers, the third as chief aircraft instrumentation engineer at the Naval Aircraft Factory—all had him stationed in or around Philadelphia. He performed his official duties during the day. But, for the first four years of that tour, "Chick" Hayward was enrolled in night classes at the University of Pennsylvania, the Moore School, and Temple University, working on advancing his career. His course selections were the clue to what that career was: mathematical analysis, experimental atomic physics, applied gyrodynamics, magnetism, among a handful of other subjects.

After making the 25,000th aircraft landing on the Franklin D. Roosevelt, *Hayward is escorted to the bridge by the carrier's commanding officer, Captain Walter E. Clarke.*
(National Archives)

Military Leaders Since World War II

For nearly three years after the Japanese attack on Pearl Harbor, he put aside his career-option plan of becoming a nuclear physicist, and went to war. The last part of that period, from May 1943 through June 1944, Hayward commanded a bombing squadron in the Pacific. His team not only bombed enemy shipping and shore-based staging areas, it also scouted targets for the surface fleet. Arleigh Burke, then in command of the Little Beavers, met Hayward that way, over the radio.

"Particularly on 'Black Cat' [night call]," said Burke, "we got to be very good friends with people we'd never seen; spotters who could find the enemy for us so we could do the damage. Most importantly, they could find out where the enemy was being reinforced from." In addition, during just one two-month stretch in 1944, Hayward's squadron sank 26 enemy cargo vessels and barges, damaged 23 more, and shot down a dozen Japanese aircraft. When Hayward was ordered to the Naval Ordnance Test Station, Inyokern, California, in July 1944, he brought with him a Silver Star, Legion of Merit, four Distinguished Flying Crosses, five Air Medals, and a Purple Heart.

The test facility at Inyokern was less than a year old when Hayward arrived there as its first formally titled experimental officer. During the next nine years, he would change his mailing address a lot: to director of plans and operations for the Armed Forces Special Weapons (atomic) project (AFSWP) at Sandia Base, Albuquerque, New Mexico (1947–1948); then commander of Composite Squadron Five (to mid-1951); then head of weapons research at the Atomic Energy Commission in Washington, D.C., until May 1953.

For the first six of those years, he also pressed on with his own higher education. From 1944 to 1946 at the California Institute of Technology (CalTech), for instance, he studied such subjects as exterior and interior ballistics of rockets, chemistry of explosives and solid propellants, optics, microtime physics. At the University of New Mexico and at Los Alamos (1947–1948), he studied physics of the atmosphere; wave mechanics; uranium, plutonium, and nuclear processes. At Stanford University (1949), Hayward studied more of the same.

But, Hayward's mission for most of those nine years was to create a Navy capable of delivering nuclear weapons from carrier-based aircraft. Particularly among younger officers who, like Hayward, knew both carrier tactics and nuclear science, the Navy simply would be a poor player in deterring, or winning, future wars if it failed to modernize itself. The technology available to do that was not much of a mystery. Engineering it into the fleet was. Existing Navy carrier-based aircraft simply couldn't carry the payload, and existing Navy carriers weren't strong enough to handle heavy bombers, or large enough to permit night operations in bad weather.

Then, of course, there was the politics, the bitter contest in the Pentagon, White House, and Congress over letting the Navy have a piece, in effect, of the Air Force's atomic monopoly. In short, the Navy would have to prove its carrier was a wise option to Air Force strategic bombers for nuclear-weapons delivery; and, at the same time, that the carrier, itself, was not an easy target for atomic attack. Even within the Navy, faith in those claims was not unanimous. Nor was Hayward at all certain his lowly commander's career would survive his helping sell that program to much higher authority.

Today, the facility at Inyokern is called the Naval Weapons Center, China Lake, California. With 6,000 employees, more than one million acres of test range, it is the Navy's largest research, development, and test/evaluation complex. It was not that for Hayward in 1944. Prior to flying to China Lake, Hayward stopped at CalTech to meet top scientists whose projects would require the resources he had to provide.

Then, he flew on to China Lake. "I was real upset with the assignment," he said. "I thought I'd done a real good job at the war and I wanted to stay with it." His first look at Inyokern didn't make him feel any better. "As I pulled up over Red Rock Canyon, I saw nothing; I mean *literally* nothing: a single air-strip, six galvanized metal quonset huts, a mess hall, and a lot of dust in the middle where people were building things."

Hayward had been at China Lake for a year when a new base commander, Captain James B. Sykes, arrived. Whatever else he might have been, Sykes was an expert on Navy regulations. He ordered Hayward to stop allowing CalTech civilians to ride Navy buses from their China Lake housing to work, and to ban "female civilians" from Navy aircraft commuting between China Lake and CalTech. Commander Hayward then, from his own office, called Washington to announce, "China Lake has been shut down." After he had explained why, the head of Naval Research, the head of the Atomic Energy Commisison, and Navy Secretary James V. Forrestal all called Sykes to "straighten him out"—and gave Hayward a temporary promotion to captain.

For Hayward, the whole incident reinforced the fifth of the five character traits for excellent leadership told to him by Vice Admiral Marc A. "Pete" Mitscher, a stronger backer of China Lake. The five include: (1) Knowledge of the subject; (2) Self-confidence, which is helped by knowledge; (3) Enthusiasm for the job; (4) Integrity, including frank, honest reports to superior officers; and (5) Judgment, "which 'Uncle Pete' said," according to Hayward, "meant knowing when to 'intelligently disregard regulations.' "

Noted one of China Lake's engineers, J. D. Gerrard-Gough, "Chick Hayward was a very human character, who not only was predisposed to buck the system when it slowed down progress; but also was a grand master at that particular science." In a way, Sykes endorsed that view in the only negative efficiency report (ER) Hayward ever received from a commanding officer. Said Sykes, "He was more knowledgeable than I was on technical things; but he was not concerned with orderliness or the regulations."

A hint to the pain that caused him, both personally and professionally, can be found in his personal diary's entry for March 21, 1951: "Time alone will sit in judgment as to how well I did my job in helping bring the Navy into the atomic weapons era. In years to come, I hope to see the Navy really accept this new role in modern warfare." It did, eventually. By the mid-1950s, after a series of often nasty setbacks, supercarriers were being built. So was the first generation of carrier-based aircraft for handling nuclear weapons the way they are today, as routine carrier operations.

By then, and for the remainder of his career, Hayward was wrapped up in other important Navy projects. He served one five-year tour, for instance, as CNO Arleigh Burke's first Deputy CNO for research and development. There, he helped develop the Navy's anti-submarine warfare (ASW) tactics and technology, reportedly the world's best today.

In 1962, Hayward accepted a temporary demotion to rear admiral so he could command the Navy's first nuclear-powered carrier, the *Enterprise*, on her maiden voyage. He also was in command of her, off the Cuban coast, during the October 1962 Cuban missile crisis. Basically, he was staying with the creations he had fostered in tactical air operations and in ASW, learning what the sailors who have to use them think. (Noting his *Enterprise* task force could circle the earth nonstop, he added, "That's why sailors hate the nuclear Navy; they never get any shore leave.")

The military's top non-combat award is the Distinguished Service Medal. Hayward had received two by the time he retired: one for his ASW work, the other for his contributions to education. Technology experts, that unique combination of awards suggests, need to be effective teachers, as well. Some experts on military affairs say Hayward's greatest contribution to the modern Navy was his pioneering leadership in ASW. Others insist it was his scientific and engineering expertise, directing the modernization of Navy aircraft carriers and other surface ships so they could handle nuclear bombs and missiles efficiently and effectively.

But future historians may decide his finest contribution was helping build the Naval War College into the excellent, graduate-level institution it is today. That, after all, is a final academic testing ground for some Army, some Air Force, and a large number of future Navy and Marine Corps leaders.

Chronology

November 15, 1908	John Tucker Hayward born in New York City
1925	enlists in the Navy
1926	enters the U.S. Naval Academy, graduating in 1930
1932	earns his naval aviator's wings at Pensacola Naval Air Station, Pensacola, Florida
1943	organizes on the West Coast, then commands in South Pacific combat action a patrol/bomber squadron; is promoted to commander
1947	named director of plans and operations at Sandia Base, Albuquerque, New

	Mexico; promoted to permanent rank of captain while there
1951	is assigned to the Atomic Energy Commission
1957–1962	assigned to the office of the Chief of Naval Operations (CNO) as, first, director of strategic plans and, for the last three years, deputy CNO for development; is promoted to rear admiral, then vice admiral while on this tour
1962–1966	takes command of Carrier Division Two during the Cuban missile blockade (in October 1962); then assigned command of Anti-Submarine Warfare Force, Pacific
1966	named president of the Naval War College, at his request, and serves there until his retirement in September, 1968. Today, he and his wife divide their time between a home in Florida and one in Newport, Rhode Island

Decorations: in addition to unit, campaign, and foreign-government citations, Hayward holds 2DSM, SS, LM for valor, 4DFC, 5AM, PH, CR, Navy League's Adm. W. S. Parsons scientific award, and first military recipient of the Robert D. Conrad science award.

Further Reading

By John Hayward

Hayward, John Tucker, VAdm. "Chaplains Corps." In the "Oral History program," Oral History Department, U.S. Naval Institute, Annapolis, MD 21402.

Vice Admiral John T. Hayward

Hayward, John T. "Chick," Adm. In the "Oral History program," Oral History Department, U.S. Naval Institute, Annapolis, MD 21402.

About John Hayward

Davis, Vincent. *The Politics of Innovation: Patterns in Navy Cases*, Volume 4, Monograph No. 3, 1966–67. Denver, Colo: University of Denver.

Gallico, Paul. "The Dropout Who Made It to the Top," *Reader's Digest*, November 1966.

Gerrard-Gough, J. D. and Albert B. Christman. *The Grand Experiment at Inyokern*. Washington, D.C.: Government Printing Office/Naval History Division, 1978.

Hattendorf, John B. *Sailors and Scholars: A Centennial History of the U.S. Naval War College*. Newport, R.I.: Naval War College Press, 1984.

General Lewis W. Walt

On helicopter reconnaissance, Marines called Walt's cornflower blue eyes the "Twin Blues that'll knock you over if he's mad."
(National Archives)

At the Marine Barracks in downtown Washington, D.C., every Friday evening during the summer, the Marine Corps performs a "retreat" open to the public. All seats are reserved weeks in advance for the retreat's panoply of full-dress parade, a concert from the Marine Corps band, and demonstration of silent, close-order drill by a rifle platoon.

Many of the young Marines there are wearing at least a half-dozen combat medals and campaign ribbons. Their most honored guest, whenever he shows up, is the one who carries the Marines'

General Lewis W. Walt

most valued title of all: "A Marine's Marine." Lewis B. "Chesty" Puller inspired that high praise by his battlefield heroics in World War II and Korea. When he retired, he passed the title on to Lewis William Walt.

It was a remarkable achievement, particularly since Walt "had hardly heard of them," he said, when he was offered a Marine Corps commission in 1936. Walt had been born on a farm near Harveyville, Kansas, in February 1913, the seventh of 13 children. By the time he was 16, he was an orphan, living in Fort Collins, Colorado, working his way through high school as, among other things, a member of the Colorado National Guard. He would resign from the Guard as a first sergeant six years later.

Meanwhile in 1932, he entered Colorado State University (a college, then), and enlisted in its Army ROTC (Reserve Officers Training Corps) program. While working his way through four years of college, he did just about everything else there, too. When he graduated in 1936, with a bachelor of science degree in chemistry, his college biography said that he had been elected his class president two years, president of the student body and student council his senior year. He had thrown the javelin on the track team, and was the school's heavyweight entry on and captain of the wrestling team. He had played both tackle and all-conference guard on and was co-captain of the football team. He had been captain of the ROTC Scabbard and Blade fraternity and a lieutenant colonel in the ROTC program. He had been president of the chemistry club, whose membership included only the academic top 10% of the college's chemistry students.

When he graduated he had a batch of job options, despite the Great Depression. E. I. DuPont had offered him a job as a chemist. The Chicago Bears football team had offered him a tryout. His former high school coach and Sunday school teacher had offered him a job at the Colorado School of Mines as an assistant football coach. And he had a second lieutenant's commission in the Army Field Artillery Reserve as the result of the Colorado State ROTC program. Then a Marine Corps recruiter called, offering him a second lieutenant's commission in the Corps.

Walt went to the president of the university for advice. That professor said he didn't know much about the Marines except that, "They place a lot of emphasis on leadership." Then, said Walt later, "He opened the Bible on his desk, found the Scripture he was looking for, and read to me, 'He who would be first among you

Walt with South Vietnam Army 2nd Division commander Major General Nguyen Van Toan, at on-site inspection near the DMZ.
(National Archives)

must be the servant of all.' That," said Walt, "has been my guide all my life. If you're going to lead them, you've got to serve them. If you serve them, they'll take care of you."

Many years later, Marine Corps Major General R. G. Davis, former Marine Corps assistant chief of staff for manpower planning, would summarize, "I remember reports on Lew Walt as a company commander, up through battalion, regiment, division, whatever level. 'Outstanding,' they all said. He had a fine appreciation for how to get the most out of people, weapons and units. And that's what tactics is all about."

The first week of July 1936, Walt resigned his Army commission; told E. I. DuPont he would get back to them "in three or four years"; passed on the coaching job and the pro-football tryout;[1] and became a second lieutenant in the Marine Corps. His first tour was, of course, boot camp. Looking back, Walt would note, "I was extremely fortunate during those nine months to have as a platoon

---

[1]That was no great sacrifice. Even the "all-pro" players then, in what is now the National Football League, were paid only about $5,000 a season.

leader one of America's finest Marines, General Lewis 'Chesty' Puller, I learned much from him on how to be a good Marine and a leader in the Corps." Walt graduated with an honors report card from Puller.

After basic, Walt spent his next four years as a platoon leader in several places. One was San Diego, another was Guam. Also, in 1937–38, his platoon helped defend a community of Americans and other non-Chinese living together in an international community in Shanghai, China. (Having launched into China from Manchuria in what eventually became World War II in the Far East, the Japanese were threatening the city.) By the end of 1941, Walt had completed the six-month officer candidates' course at the Marine Corps Schools, Quantico, Virginia, and been promoted to captain. At the start of 1942, Walt volunteered to join the newly formed First Marine Raider Battalion, which was headed for Samoa in the South Pacific.

After five months of training, on August 7, 1942, Walt led Company A of the First Marines in the first amphibious assault on Tulagi Island, headquarters for Japanese troops on Tulagi, Florida, and Guadalcanal in the Solomon Islands chain. (Depending on the mission, a company consists of about 150–200 troops, a battalion about 700–800.) Walt was awarded a Silver Star for "conspicuous gallantry" his first day in battle.

From then until December 1944, when he was sent back to the Marine Corps Schools to teach new Marines what he had learned in war, his combat record reads like a movie script for "Rambo." He was promoted to major in September 1942; then, on Guadalcanal, received an on-the-spot promotion to lieutenant colonel from the First Marine Division commander. He was recommended for the Navy Cross three times and received it twice.[2] "Silent Lew," as he was known then, spent 1943 in a hospital in Melbourne, Australia and four months in early 1944 at the naval hospital in Oakland, California, recovering from wounds and malaria.

Eight years later, after promotion to colonel in November 1951, he would repeat most of that performance in the Korean War. By the time he served there, from November 1952, until August 1953, it had degenerated into the "no win, no peace" war that angered the troops—and inflamed most of the American people back home. Commander of the Fifth Marine Regiment, then First

---

[2]Since "unification" of the armed forces in 1947, both the Navy Cross and Air Force Cross have the same title: Distinguished Service Cross. Whatever its name, the only combat award that outranks it is the congressional Medal of Honor.

Marine Division chief of staff, he also ended up with both the Legion of Merit and a Bronze Star, both with combat "V" for valor.

Said the Division commanding officer, in the Legion of Merit citation, "Through [Walt's] exceptional knowledge of friendly, as well as enemy, military tactics, he [was] capable and resourceful . . . in repulsing numerous attempts by the enemy to penetrate the main line of resistance." The tactic he used, in that stalemate war, to prevent a flood of Chinese troops from overwhelming one of his outposts, was to attack it, to bust it up before it could mobilize. His medals notwithstanding, Walt left Korea convinced thousands of American lives had been sacrificed to what he thought of as "traitors" and "idiots" back in Washington, D.C.

"In Korea," he wrote after he had retired in February 1971, "we were required to submit an attack plan 24 hours in advance. I was particularly upset that the Chinese enemy seemed to know when and where the attack was coming. So, we could not achieve surprise." He complained at the time, too, about the possibility of spies in the chain of command; but no formal military investigation of the charge ever was started.

Most of Walt's career, when he was not fighting in World War II, Korea, or Vietnam, was spent outside the public limelight at the Marine Corps Schools in Quantico, Virginia. All told, he spent more than one-third of his 35-year military career working at the schools in one leadership role or another. Twice he was head of tactics training. He also was battalion commander in a Special Training Regiment; graduated from the Senior Course on Amphibious Warfare; was a top faculty member of the Education Center twice; was director of the Landing Force Development Center; and finally, was the commanding officer of the Basic School.

That last assignment he considered "the highlight of my career, one of the really great challenges an officer can experience. In that position you have such a lasting and long-range effect on the entire Corps. You feel a heavy responsibility because the caliber of officer you turn out is going to determine to a large extent the caliber of the Marine Corps. It's a tremendous experience working with these young men, building leaders as well as tacticians."

Promoted to brigadier general in 1962, he was promoted again, to major general in May 1965, one month before he was sent to Vietnam. There, he was promoted to lieutenant general in March 1966; and, when he left Vietnam in June 1967, he called that tour "the most challenging job I ever had." Walt's territorial responsibility was I ("Eye") Corps, a 3,000-square-mile area extending south from the Demilitarized Zone (DMZ), the official boundary between North and South Vietnam. Within that Corps area, Walt commanded some 73,000 Marines and about 7,000 Army, Navy, and Air Force personnel. He was also senior adviser to 70,000 South Vietnamese troops and ultimately responsible for the safety of some 2.5 million South Vietnamese civilians living in the I Corps area.

Walt's career record said he was an outstanding combat leader. In Vietnam, he also demonstrated great skills at policy-level planning and decision-making, a brand of leadership expected at the Pentagon level but not often seen on the battlefield. In this case, at the outset of his Vietnam assignment, he realized both the enemy's strategy, and how best to defeat it.

"In this war," he said simply, "the people have always been the objective. If we can assure them protection, the people will do the rest. In essence, what we are doing is fighting a war and at the same time trying to rebuild a nation."

Within two months after his arrival in Vietnam, Walt had begun to organize combined action platoons (CAPs), squad-sized units assigned to live in the "villies," as the troops called the villages. The Marines' tasks there were to defend the villagers from nighttime raids by Communist guerrillas; escort the villagers to market with their rice crops during the day; and train the "villies'" Popular Forces (PFs) of from 15 to 30 militia in patrol tactics and the use of small arms to defend themselves.

Soon, the CAPs were organized under CACs (combined action companies), so they could work together, providing coverage to several neighborhood villages at once. Then, the CACs were pulled together under CAGs (combined action groups) for the same reason. In late 1965, when Walt's CAP program started, 87 villages, some 400,000 people, were rated "secure" from Communist assault. When Walt left Vietnam in 1967, 197 villages and one million Vietnamese civilians were deemed "secure."

An even more dramatic endorsement of the program came from Walt's CAP Marines, themselves. In total at its peak, the CAP strategy involved 42 officers, more than 2,000 enlisted Marines, plus two Navy officers and 126 medical corpsmen. When their mandatory one-year tour in Vietnam ended, more than 50% of them volunteered to extend for one more year. Though their work never appeared on national television, it was, said Walt, "the heart-warming, humane side of the war, Marines helping Vietnamese build or rebuild schools, churches, roads, plant and harvest rice, set up orphanages and medical clinics. Our Marines of today," he added, "have been the finest young ambassadors America has ever put into any country, certainly on any battlefield."

During his two years in Vietnam, Walt logged as much as 10,000 helicopter miles a month, on the deck at 120 knots an hour, often drawing enemy sniper fire as he surveyed combat positions and visited his soldiers. Because of that, they nicknamed him "The Three-Star Grunt" and "The Great Squad Leader in the Sky." Said one combat veteran, "The Marine in Vietnam who did not tend toward hero worship of Walt was hard to find."

That feeling was not shared everywhere, by any means. Walt's popularity plummeted in the Pentagon, for instance, when he called "foolhardy" a decision by the secretary of defense to build an electronic "detection barrier" the length of the DMZ. He also resisted an order to tone down his CAP program and attack large North Vietnamese troop concentrations, instead. CAP was vital, answered Walt, and he didn't have enough Marines to do both that and fight a conventional war, too.

I Corps Marines give their "Three-Star Grunt" a lift up.
(National Archives)

General Lewis W. Walt

The result of the debates was that Walt was ordered back to Marine Corps headquarters in Washington, D.C. as director of personnel, a lowly task for not only a lieutenant general, but the most experienced combat veteran in the Marine Corps. In the end, Walt was the winner, sort of, in these contests. For one thing, he received two Distinguished Service Medals during the remaining four years of his career. Both were linked, either directly or indirectly, to his service in Vietnam and the CAP program. He was appointed Marine Corps assistant commandant in January 1968; and, as a result of a specific, new congressional law, became the first assistant commandant promoted to four-star rank.

Concluded Lt. Colonel James D. Rogers who was Army liaison to Walt's command in Vietnam, "It was during his two-year assignment in Vietnam that Walt's name became synonymous with his Marines in combat." In return, after he retired, Walt became one of their strongest public defenders. His message, in brief:

There is indeed no substitute for victory; nor can a nation such as ours, which depends on the citizen-soldier, commit its sons and daughters to a no-win war without inflicting unbearable and lasting damage on their morale and military effectiveness. Our sons and daughters are patriots, not mercenaries. Patriots can not be asked to endure the horrors of war except to accomplish a goal which is equivalent in value to life, itself.

Since the end of World War II, U.S. military forces have fought in two major wars and some "minor" ones—minor in that they lasted only a month or less. Military teams also have been used several times to counterattack against terrorists and drug smugglers. None of these costly contests was preceded, as in the old war-fighting manner, by a formal declaration of war. Interestingly enough, the Marine Corps has been fighting these kinds of undeclared wars ever since its founding in 1775—one year before the signing of the Declaration of Independence. To maintain combat readiness, and the flexibility to handle any assignment, is particularly difficult under these circumstances. The Marine Corps record is overflowing with evidence of its unexcelled ability to do that.

The principal reason they have, and can, has little to do with high-technology weapons or exotic electronic command and control systems. Instead, the Marine Corps emphasis is, as it always has been, on people, their pride in doing well what they

Military Leaders Since World War II

do, their morale, *Semper Fidelis*, as the Marine Corps motto says. Such a winning attitude, as coaches say in school, does not come automatically.

In the Marine Corps, the leader valued most is not the one who adapts best to change in technology, in nuclear strategy, in international politics. The best military leader is the one who simply passes on to the next generation a winning attitude. Whether teaching at the Marine Corps Schools or leading troops in combat, Lew Walt, "The Marines' Marine," did that.

Chronology

February 16, 1913	Lewis William Walt born near Harveyville, Kansas
1936	graduates from Colorado State University, accepts a second lieutenant's commission in the Marine Corps
1939	promoted to first lieutenant while in Guam, having served already in San Diego and Shanghai, China
1941	completes courses at Marine Corps Schools, Quantico, Virginia, and is promoted to captain
1942–1944	commands combat units in the Solomon Islands; in 1942, is promoted to major in September, then lieutenant colonel in December; hospitalized in Australia in 1943; spends 1944 in combat except for four months in a hospital in Oakland, California
1951	promoted to colonel, serves on staff at the Marine Corps Schools
1953	completes 21 months combat duty in the Korean War

1957	completes service as commander, Officers Basic School, Marine Corps Schools
1960	graduates from the National War College, is promoted to brigadier general one year later
1965–1967	serves two years in Vietnam with promotion to major general at the beginning of that tour, promotion to lieutenant general in 1966
1968–1971	serves as Marine Corps assistant commandant, with promotion to general, until he retires in February 1971 to become an author, columnist, and lecturer. He dies of cardiac arrest in Mississippi in March 1989

Decorations: his nearly 50 medals and citations include 2DSC, 2DSM, SS, LM and BSM (both for valor), 2PH.

Further Reading

By Lewis Walt
The Eleventh Hour. Foreword by Eugene V. Rostow. Ottawa, Ill.: Caroline House Publishers, 1979.

Strange War, Strange Strategy: A General's Report on Vietnam. Foreword by President Lyndon B. Johnson. New York: Funk & Wagnalls, 1970.

About Lewis Walt
"Changing the Guard," *Newsweek*, May 29, 1967, p. 47.

Elliott, SSgt. Jim. "General Walt," *Leatherneck*, February 1971, p. 32.

"In Memoriam," *Leatherneck*, May 1989, p. 22.

Lynn, Robert A. "General Lewis W. Walt—'Uncle Lew' to his Marines—was the stuff of which legends are made," *Vietnam*, Volume 2, Number 6, p. 8.

"Lewis W. Walt, Marine Corps General, Dies at 76," *The New York Times*, March 28, 1989, p. B6.

"Marine Gen. Lewis W. Walt Dies at 76," *The Washington Post*, March 29, 1989, p. B6.

General George S. Brown

Joint Chiefs Chairman George Brown.
(U.S. Department of Defense photo)

---

*I*raqi dictator Saddam Hussein had promised, in late 1990, the "mother of all battles" if a 28-nation combat force attacked his occupation army in and around Kuwait. The coalition's air assault started on January 16, 1991; the ground attack on February 23. On February 27, President George Bush declared officially, "The war is over." Observed one Army official dryly, "The 'mother of all battles' has become the granddaddy of all victories."

Among the numbers in the final tally: 29 Iraqi divisions (some 522,000 soldiers), including about half its elite, battle-hardened Revolutionary Guard, torn to shreds; 80% of Iraq's tanks, and artillery destroyed; 103 of its combat aircraft blown apart; 63,000 of its troops in Saudi prison camps. Only 202 American and 82 allied men and women were killed or missing in action, an amazingly low number. (Coalition supreme commander, Army

General H. Norman Schwarzkopf, called that the greatest "victory" of the victory.)

When the shooting started, each side seemed to have some advantages, in numbers at least. But, "Stormin' " Norman Schwarzkopf, also had a plan. His enemy, as it turned out, seemed to have only what any city sidewalk mugger has: a weapon and a nasty attitude. Schwarzkopf's plan, Joint Chiefs Chairman Colin Powell told a January 23rd press conference, was, "First, we're going to cut it off [the Iraqi Army], and then we're going to kill it."

The cut off part was handled by air power. For 38 days, starting January 16, a constant swarm of bombers, fighters armed with "smart bombs," and ship-launched Tomahawk cruise missiles, shattered Hussein's communication links with his army, blew apart combat units and supply depots, and gutted the road and rail arteries to Kuwait—the pipelines for the food, water, ammunition, fuel, and spare parts an army must have to stay alive. Hussein's reaction was to fire Scud missiles at Israeli and Saudi Arabian cities, a terrorist act of no military consequence.

Next, to destroy the Iraqi army, Schwarzkopf used a sweeping end-run, hitting it on its flank while also throwing a "Hail Mary pass," as he called it. On February 23rd, the 101st Airborne Division performed the "Hail Mary," using 300 assault helicopters to jump deep inside Iraq and block the road to Baghdad. That same day, some 240,000 U.S., British, and French troops, mostly in armored and mechanized infantry divisions, slashed in from the west at the Iraqi right flank.

That huge force, with its 60-day supply of water, ammunition, and fuel, had moved 150 or so miles west of Kuwait during just the preceding three weeks, itself an unprecedented display of military mobility. But, Schwarzkopf said later, when the Iraqi enemy didn't pivot to keep that force in front of it, "That was when I knew we had won the war." Simply put, Schwarzkopf had used tactics from the Pentagon's Air-Land Battle Doctrine, which relies upon massive firepower to stun the enemy followed by surprise attacks on its flanks and rear.

Few noted during the post-war celebrations the key role that doctrine played in the war. Pointing it out takes nothing away from Schwarzkopf's leadership. Game plans, excellent though they may be, do not win wars; people do. And, after all, thousands of coalition people had put their lives at risk on a combat doctrine never before tested in war—though it had been rehearsed for a decade by NATO forces in central Europe. Still, a complete history

General George S. Brown

MACV Commander, General Abrams (left), and his deputy for air operations, General George Brown (right), greet Joint Chiefs Chairman General Earle Wheeler, as the latter arrives in Saigon.
(National Archives)

---

of the Persian Gulf War ought to have in it at least a mention of the Air-Land Doctrine's godfathers, Army General Creighton Abrams and Air Force General George Brown.[1]

The two men first had paired up in 1968, the year Abrams became commander, MACV (Military Assistance Command, Vietnam), and Brown arrived there as commander of the Seventh Air Force and deputy MACV commander for air operations. The latter title was Brown's invention, a symbolic gesture helping create, claimed one historian, "the finest rapport and mutual trust between a ground-based theater commander and his air-subordinate since World War II." Said General Robert J. Dixon, Brown's

---

[1]Had he lived, Abrams would have had a very personal concern about the doctrine's use because, in the Persian Gulf War, one of his sons, Brigadier General Creighton Abrams, Jr., commanded the VII Corps artillery; another, Captain Bruce Abrams, commanded a tank company. (His third son, Brigadier General John N. Abrams, was Army deputy chief of staff for operations in the Pentagon.)

Vietnam vice commander for a time, "Nobody knew more about airpower than Abrams did. When somebody wanted us to brief them on the Vietnam air war, we tried to get Abrams to do it."

In 1970, Brown was transferred from Vietnam to command of the Air Force Systems Command (AFSC), the fountainhead for nearly all new Air Force aircraft, missiles, weapons, electronics, and other hardware and software. In 1972, his next-to-last year there, Abrams became Army Chief of Staff. A year later, Brown was named Air Force Chief of Staff. From what they had learned in Vietnam, they agreed both the Army and Air Force needed drastic changes in their rulebooks on how ground troops and air force pilots are supposed to work together in battle.

They ordered the Tactical Air Command (TAC) and the Army Doctrine Command to work together to produce the product. It was the beginning of a major, cage-rattling change in attitudes and priorities among the people running Army and Air Force conventional- war combat, training, and supply organizations. It meant developing and buying new military equipment and redirecting finances toward new priorities.

Knowing, at least in general terms, what hardware the Tactical Air Force would need to perform its role in the Air-Land Doctrine, Brown had not waited until Abrams' return to get AFSC working on it. Most of the "smart bombs"—"smart" because they had to be certain of hitting enemy targets, not the friendly forces nearby—went into advanced development while Brown was AFSC Commander. So did the first Air Force aircraft in 20 years designed strictly for close-air support of ground troops. So, too, did several Army–Air Force electronic command-communications projects, so soldiers and pilots could talk to each other on the same wavelength, a combat rarity in Vietnam.

The whole collection was an example of what Lawrence A. Skantze, who would become head of AFSC in the 1980s, meant when he said, "George Brown didn't have a lot of the technical science and engineering knowledge; but he had just a natural talent for knowing the right way to direct the efforts."

Forcing a basic creation like the Air-Land Battle Doctrine on entrenched organization is a very fragile matter, especially in the early stages. Abrams died in office in September 1974, cutting Air-Land's top military leadership in half. However, two months earlier, Air-Land's other main missionary, George Brown, had been elevated to chairman of the Joint Chiefs of Staff, boosting immensely his power to force the change. Thus, uniquely in

General George S. Brown

military history, the instructions were as ready as the forces themselves when the Persian Gulf War began.

Born in Montclair, New Jersey in August 1918, George Scratchley Brown was the first son of Army cavalry officer Thoburn Brown (U.S. Military Academy class of 1913) and Frances Scratchley-Brown of New York City. Typical of a military family's nomadic life, George Brown attended 9th grade in Washington, D.C., 10th grade in Texas, and the 11th and 12th grades in Leavenworth, Kansas.

Along the way, Brown became an Eagle Scout; was named all-league fullback for an inter-state high school football league; showed a talent for tennis; and developed an expert's skill as a horseman and polo player. (Because the army moved mostly on horseback in those days, many Army units across the country played polo.)

Largely because his father was his role model, George Brown had decided very early in his life that being a West Point cadet was the ultimate adventure. Neither of his parents wanted him to go to West Point just because his father had. Frequently, they told him of many other attractions in the world besides West Point. George was not persuaded. He did spend a year (1936–37) at the University of Missouri, studying engineering and serving in the Missouri National Guard.

But that was only an interlude while friends of his and his father's in Leavenworth, Kansas—a bank president, the owner of the town newspaper, and the owner of a local flour mill—helped him get an appointment to the U.S. Military Academy. He entered in 1937—and failed both French and mathematics at the end of his first semester. If he also failed the make-up exams at the end of his second semester, he was told, he would be dismissed from school. He studied nearly six months, without a vacation break, preparing for those tests.

Classmates helped, at times after "Taps" when people not in bed are slapped with demerits. They ran the risk, some of them said later, in part because they already had designated him a future Army leader. Summed up one classmate, Ed Rowny "Cadets are always guessing who in class will become Army Chief of Staff. Brown was a marked man at a very early date." Brown's senior-year roommate, First Captain of Cadets Jack Norton, agreed.

"I think George's pursuit of academics was sort of a necessary function with him; one he had to pursue," said Norton. "He eventually did well enough, but it was in military tactics that

George Brown really found himself, ending up one of the top three or four student-officers in class." But he did not equal that rank in the classroom. When he graduated from West Point, in June 1941, he was ranked 342nd in a class of 424.

The year before, his grandfather, H. P. Scratchley, had written to him: "I know that the young do not like to be preached to however much the old like to preach. But there is no higher type of man in this world than the Christian gentleman who does his duty in the sight of God without fear. May you be this. The existence of what America stands for is in the hands of your generation. May God give of his power to do your duty rightly in this darkening world." He had that letter with him when he became Joint Chiefs Chairman 34 years later.

By the time his turn came to pick a career specialty, the only options left were infantry and quartermaster corps. He picked the infantry—and applied for flight training, the closest he could come to following his father into the cavalry. The Army Air Corps collared him immediately, and this time his classroom grades were well above average. He had to become a bomber pilot only because he was two inches taller than the 5-foot, 10-inch maximum height the Air Corps would allow for a fighter pilot. He was in Europe by September 1942, after three months of flying the B-24 *Liberator* bomber on anti-submarine missions out of Florida.

His most life-threatening flight in World War II was on August 1, 1943. That Sunday, 178 B-24s, including the 40 in his 93rd Bomb Group, left Libya on a 2,400-mile, round-trip flight to bomb Ploesti, Rumania's oil fields and refineries, the well-head for two-thirds of Nazi Germany's gasoline and engine oil. Brown took charge of his group when its group commander's aircraft was shot down; and led the 93rd Bomb Group's 29 aircraft that survived the raid back to Libya.

He earned a Distinguished Service Cross then, and later a superior's comment that he was, "An exceptionally intelligent, capable, and forceful young officer whose leadership, judgment and common sense have been developed far beyond his years." (He was 25 at the time.) In England next, the 93rd joined the 8th Air Force flying daylight raids over Germany. At the end of the war, Brown was a 2nd Bomb Division operations officer. The briefest summary of Brown's World War II leadership may have come from his wife, Alice "Skip" Brown. "When he went to war in 1942," she said, "he was a second lieutenant. The next time I saw him, three years later, he was a colonel."

From May 1945, when he returned to the United States, until August 1959, when he finally was promoted to brigadier general, Colonel Brown covered the Air Force flying field. He held down assignments in command or as a commander's operations assistant, in flight training commands, fighter-interceptor wings, and air-transport groups. He began one four-year cycle (1950–1953) commanding the Korean airlift, an emergency transport of troops and equipment from the West Coast after the North Koreans attacked the South in June 1950. He ended that cycle in the Korean War itself, directing flight operations of the Fifth Tactical Air Force.

After graduation from the National War College in 1957, he was called across the Potomac River into the Pentagon to be executive officer to Air Force Chief of Staff Thomas D. White. "I knew nothing about the Pentagon or how to get anything done there," Brown told a biographer later. "I didn't even know where to get a cup of coffee."

White, on the other hand, he added, "just had no fear. He knew how the games were played in this town, how the work went on." He understood the rivalries within the Pentagon, and between it and other government agencies. White had one leadership talent Brown also would master by the time he became Air Force Chief of Staff. "White believed in persuasion, not confrontation. He'd pass up a short-term gain on some issue if a 'victory' then would provoke, within the bureaucracy, an 'enemy' who later could wreck what White believed was a critical long-range program."

Most of the time from then until he was sent to Vietnam in August 1968, Brown's assignments put him in very delicate, career-threatening positions. He was giving either a secretary of defense, as his military assistant, or the chairman of the Joint Chiefs of Staff, as his secretary, an honest, personal view on an issue, an opinion often contrary to the ambitions of his parent military service.

He sided with his boss, Secretary of Defense Thomas S. Gates, Jr., for instance, in Gates' creation of the Joint Strategic Planning Group, a single organization that would make all the targeting decisions on all nuclear weapons regardless of whether the Navy or the Air Force had some of the individual weapons themselves. Pentagon leadership in both the Air Force and Navy were vehemently opposed to Gates' decision at the time. He also sided with his boss, Secretary of Defense Robert S. McNamara, in canceling development of the B-70 bomber, a proposition Air Force leaders bitterly and publicly fought against.

Concluded McNamara, in what turned out to be a typical testimonial to Brown's career, "He had high intelligence, broad experience, and sensitivity to military-foreign policy issues. But most of all he had absolute integrity. The job required that and Brown had it. He was never reluctant to disagree with me—which he did often." McNamara said at the time that he thought Brown was qualified to be chairman of the Joint Chiefs of Staff.

Though Brown trod on a lot of sensitive toes in his "joint service work," as the Pentagon calls it, during the 1960s, that didn't seem to have hurt his rate of promotion. He was promoted to brigadier general in August 1959, two months after he first went to work for Gates; was boosted to major general in April 1963 after having worked for McNamara for more than two years; became a lieutenant general in August 1966 when he became secretary to the chairman of the Joint Chiefs of Staff, Army General Earle W.

General George Brown being sworn in as Air Force Chief of Staff. Secretary of Defense James Schlesinger is at far left.
(Official USAF photo)

General George S. Brown

Wheeler; and a four-star general in August 1968 when he was sent to Vietnam.

He also had earned very high grades as both a combat-command leader and an excellent staff officer, a rare combination. While Brown was Air Force Chief of Staff and Joint Chiefs chairman, said Dixon, "George Brown worked every problem as hard as it could be worked. He pushed as hard as any sensible person should. Push too hard and you generate opposition you wouldn't otherwise have. He was excellent, steering all the time that fine line between being a tough tactician and being tactful."

It was well-known that Brown favored development of the B-1 bomber when newly elected President Jimmy Carter canceled it, fulfilling an election-campaign promise. At the time, an irate congressman demanded, "Why don't you resign?" Answered Brown, "I certainly could, but it would have about as much effect on this country as you resigning from Congress." Privately, he added, "What good would it do any of these key programs if I get fired and am never heard from again?"

He did manage to keep research going on the B-1 in spite of President Carter's decision. He saved the North American Air Defense Command (NORAD) in much the same way when higher, civilian authority wanted to abolish it. (Brown got approval to have the Air National Guard run most NORAD operations as the Navy, for years, has had its "weekend warriors" fly most U.S.-coastline anti-submarine warfare missions.)

Brown also went head-on to protect other programs of long-term value. One hardball debate he won was against threats in Congress to scrap the AWACS (Airborne Warning and Control System). Dozens of air-ground actions, including the Persian Gulf War, might have turned out far differently if he had failed.

Brown also showed he could move hard and fast in military command if he had to. The most dramatic time was in October 1973, when Egypt and Syria attacked Israel during Yom Kippur. Air Force Chief of Staff Brown had the weekend duty that Sunday night as acting chairman of the Joint Chiefs. He promptly ordered U.S. fighter aircraft and transports loaded with military resupply out of Europe to Israel.

In the process, he overruled a secretary of state's order forbidding arms shipments to Israel, and usurped presidential authority to make that kind of decision. The resupply, the Israeli prime minister would announce a year later, probably saved Israel's life. Amazingly, after issuing his unprecedented orders, Brown left town on vacation. General Lucius Clay, for one, was not surprised. "George was unique. He had the ability to make a decision, decentralize the execution of it, and then walk off, saying, 'Do your job.'"

Under the circumstances, it seems particularly ironic that, a year later and again in 1976, a leading Washington, D.C. newspaper charged him with being anti-Semitic. The cause of the first charge was a comment he made at an off-the-record session with Duke University students. The second resulted from an off-the-record interview with an "Israeli photographer," who actually was a U.S. newspaper reporter. Original interview transcripts in both cases argue that the subsequent newspaper headlines were highly creative interpretations of what Brown actually said.

Brown did kick himself, privately. "Off the record or not," he said, "there are some things a person in my position simply can't say—even when they're true." Commented one 40-year veteran reporter, "George Brown was such a modest, self-effacing guy, and Washington, D.C., is such a cruel, cut-throat bureaucracy. I can explain how he became Chairman of the Joint Chiefs of Staff, but I don't understand it."

As his friend Army General Creighton Abrams had in September 1974, Brown died of cancer in December 1978. During his last five years on active duty, Brown had been Air Force Chief of Staff when Admiral Tom Moorer was chairman of the Joint Chiefs of Staff, and had succeeded Moorer as chairman in August 1974. Claimed Moorer, a dozen years later, "George Brown was one of the best Air Force generals of that era, from the Vietnam buildup in 1964 to his retirement in 1978."

Chronology

August 17, 1918 George Scratchley Brown born in Montclair, New Jersey

General George S. Brown

1941	graduates from the U.S. Military Academy
1942–1944	completes bomber pilot training, then spends the rest of World War II planning and leading bomber missions out of Libya and, mostly, England; is promoted up through the ranks during the war from first lieutenant to, in October 1944, colonel
1952	assigned to direct Fifth Tactical Air Force operations in the Korean War
1953	assigned command of pilot training at Williams Air Force Base, Arizona
1957	graduates from the National War College
1959	becomes military assistant to the Secretary of Defense, and is promoted to brigadier general
1963	promoted to major general and assigned command of the East Coast division of the Military Air Transport Command
1966	promoted to lieutenant general, named assistant to the chairman, Joint Chiefs of Staff
1968	promoted to general, assigned command of the Seventh Tactical Air Force and, concurrently, deputy MACV commander for air operations, Vietnam
1970	assigned command of the Air Force Systems Command, headquartered at Andrews Air Force Base, Maryland
1973	named Air Force Chief of Staff
1974–1978	serves as chairman of the Joint Chiefs of Staff; dies of cancer in December 1978, six months after retirement

Decorations: his four-dozen medals, awards, and citations include a DSC, DDSM, 4DSM, SS, 3LM, 2DFC, BSM, CR, JSCM, 4AM.

Further Reading

By George Brown

Brown, General George S., USAF; Chairman, Joint Chiefs of Staff, 1974–1978. *Addresses and Statements*. Washington, D.C.: Historical Division, Joint Chiefs of Staff, 1979.

About George Brown

"Decision Maker," *Government Executive*, April 1971, pp. 32–33.

"Gen. George Brown Dies; Headed Joint Chiefs," *The Washington Post*, December 6, 1978, p. A 20.

"National Security: Spending in Perspective," *Government Executive*, March 1975, p. 26.

Puryear, Edgar F. *George S. Brown, General, U.S. Air Force: Destined for the Stars*. Novato, Calif.: Presidio Press, 1983.

"Strategic Nuclear Balance is Not Enough," *Government Executive*, December 1967, p. 24.

Webb, Willard J. and Ronald H. Cole. *The Chairman of the Joint Chiefs of Staff*. Washington, D.C.: Historical Division, Joint Chiefs of Staff, 1989, p. 89.

Lieutenant General James A. Abrahamson

SDI Project Director Abrahamson.
(Department of Defense photo)

Watching the Persian Gulf War on television in early 1991, most people were fascinated by the display of American "new" high-technology weapons. Films of the first air attacks, for instance, showed camera-guided Maverick missiles blasting with surgical precision through a doorway or rooftop air vent into an Iraqi tank bunker or command post. Maverick wasn't new high-tech at all. It's a 20-year-old weapon produced initially in the early 1970s when Air Force Lieutenant Colonel James Alan Abrahamson was Maverick program director.

Further, the mostly 20-year-old technology of Army's Patriot anti-ballistic missile (ABM) scored an impressive record, hitting Soviet-made, short-range (500 miles) Iraqi Scud missiles. That performance was blessed by the unarmed civilians in the Scud target cities, Tel Aviv, Riyadh, and Dharan. From 1984 to 1989, while he was head of the strategic defense initiative (SDI), called "Star Wars" by some, Lieutenant General Abrahamson also helped Patriot reach the Persian Gulf.

He managed the latter through a maneuver that top people in the federal government call "budget gamesmanship." Since 1983, SDI budget requests have been slashed often by a skeptical Congress. In theory, Patriot is a member of the SDI's ABM family. However, "because of the political mess in Congress," said Abrahamson, he insulated Patriot's development from the rest of SDI, thus protecting it from SDI budget cuts. One result, he noted in 1991, was that "Patriot was there, thank God. [Iraqi dictator Saddam] Hussein's psychological warfare might have succeeded, otherwise." In addition, Abrahamson hopes, "Now, everybody knows these things will work."

By the time Abrahamson retired in January 1989, he was very adept at budgeting maneuvers, and at most of the other management skills a high-tech military program director needs to deliver a product on time within budget. Like combat commanders, a program manager has to defeat adversaries and enlist allies. The difference being that most of these adversaries and allies are dozens of other program managers, all competing for limited funds, for use of the Defense Department's basic engineering and industrial personnel and facilities, and even for office space.

Moreover, the most potentially powerful new programs usually are both the most expensive and most risky because they're generally beyond the tested frontier of new scientific and engineering knowledge. Such a combination attracts volunteers—mainly from the Pentagon and Congress—who feel the need to tell the program manager, constantly, how to run his program. To perform well under all these pressures requires a particularly rare talent. Said one colleague when Abrahamson retired, "He is probably, in the program management business, the most innovative guy I know; a paragon at dreaming up ways to get things done."[1]

Being an Air Force businessman is not what Abrahamson had in mind, exactly, when he was growing up. His parents, both descendants of Norwegian immigrants, were living in Williston,

---

[1]Statement by General Lawrence A. Skantze, who was a program director and commanded the Air Force Systems Command (AFSC) from 1984 through 1987, and was Air Force vice chief of staff, as well.

Lieutenant General James A. Abrahamson

North Dakota when he was born in 1933. The family moved to Portland, Oregon while he was in first grade. His father built a profitable small business there. "We weren't rich by any means," says Abrahamson, "but we weren't poor, either."

Abrahamson, an only child, was a top student, and very active outside the classroom. About the only high school activity he didn't try was joining a fraternity. "They were a big deal then," he says, "but I thought they were just a terrible waste of time." And his schedule didn't allow for it anyway. He was on the football and track teams; in the science club, the speech club, and student politics; in the Lutheran Church teenagers' Luther League; and president of his senior class.

And, "Like everybody else," he says, "I worked." He had a newspaper route for about six years and worked in a supermarket. He also investigated working in the circus, but two days cleaning up after the elephants persuaded him the circus was not going to give him the career he wanted. While doing all this, and more, he says, "My parents were the great shapers of my life, but they were pretty subtle. By that I mean, they gave me values, pushed me onto the right track without my ever really being terribly conscious of them doing it."

Though his mother had a high school diploma, his father did not. Yet, as one illustration of their influence, he grew up knowing they just assumed he was going to college. He decided why he would in 1948. "The talk then was all about both the horror of atomic bombs, and the promise of nuclear power as our planet's next, great energy source. Out of it all, somehow, I decided, right then, to be a nuclear physicist."

That meant an engineering school. Deciding which one and how to pay for it was his first real test, and one he neglected for quite a while. "Frankly, in Portland," he says, "I'd never really been tested in any way. Life had been pretty easy."

In the fall of 1950, he chose the Massachusetts Institute of Technology (MIT), though the equally excellent California Institute of Technology (CalTech) was much closer to home. He made that choice simply because a lecturer had told his senior class that "People who live on the West Coast should go to college on the East Coast; people on the East Coast should go to the West Coast." (Abrahamson didn't think, until later, to ask, "What are the people in the Midwest supposed to do?")

MIT accepted his enrollment application, along with a requested freshman scholarship, late the following spring—too late for him to enroll somewhere else if MIT had turned him down. "Having dodged that bullet," he says, "my high school graduation was to be a triumphant time. Then, I really screwed up." He crashed his father's car into a turning vehicle, as he raced to a party for the senior-class officers from all of Portland's eight high schools. Nobody was hurt, "but it was so stupid, so dangerous, inexcusable; and it ruined my graduation for my Dad."

He earned high marks at MIT his first year, while 25% of the 900 students in his freshman class flunked out. He hit a brick wall his sophomore year, however. One reason was what he called, "Sophomore-itis, that dread disease that deludes you into thinking you can pass without studying very hard." Another was the generally impersonal student-teacher relationship at MIT compared to that in Portland.

His high school math teacher, for one, "just inspired people, at least some of us. From geometry to algebra, she always aimed us at calculus our senior year, 'the Promised Land,' 'the Magic Kingdom.'" And his history teacher "added another dimension, really gave me a legacy for my entire life. He didn't deal only in dates and events. He transplanted us back to those times, to what people thought then and why they did what they did. It was an exciting intellectual exercise." By contrast, he claims, "MIT was a factory. They had some world famous names on the faculty, but the philosophy was, 'We're the best; we know what to teach; slug it out.'"

The third, decisive reason his sophomore year was a disaster was money. From the outset, "I didn't have any money; my parents could help some but they didn't have any money, either." His scholarship meant free freshman tuition, the only cost-saving MIT offered at the time. In short, he spent his MIT years, plus his summer vacations in Portland, working to pay for his college education. His sophomore year, he simply overdid it, taking maximum class hours while working a 40-hour week—on five different jobs, all of them at "student slave-labor wages."

"[For the] first time in my life," he says, "I'd come up against what I considered a personal failure." Unable to afford a Christmas trip home, he wrote his parents, suggesting he leave school and join the Army to serve his country in the Korean War. "My Dad was desperate to make sure I didn't quit. He persuaded me to keep going." Still, summer in Portland that year was a grim visit, "not dashed hopes but certainly concern by my parents, for

Lieutenant General James A. Abrahamson

the first time in their lives, that their son maybe wasn't quite so walk-on-water as both he and they had thought."

His junior year, Abrahamson switched his major from nuclear physics to aeronautical engineering, itself a new major at MIT. His grades improved that year, and were better yet his senior year. But, he had fallen so far behind while a sophomore, "and MIT moves very hard and fast once you get started," that his four-year grade average was mediocre. Meanwhile, he also enlisted in MIT's ROTC program, a mandatory course his first two years. His reason: "I felt, if I was going to help build the machines, I ought to know how to fly them." He chose the ROTC option simply because he couldn't pay for flying lessons. In retrospect, Abrahamson says, "ROTC was a blessing and a boon."

Upon graduation the Air Force ordered him to report to Lackland Air Force Base near San Antonio, Texas in November, to receive his second lieutenant's commission and begin pilot training. Abrahamson left for Lackland by way of the nation's capital, the Great Lakes, his home in Portland, then California. He was riding "Crazy Horse," a motorcycle his MIT roommate had sold him. Crazy Horse broke down 420 miles from Lackland. Abrahamson trudged into San Antonio late on the night before he was to report for duty, down to his last 25 cents. He managed, anyway, to get his soiled uniform cleaned and an officer's stripe sewn onto it for his swearing-in. Given his MIT experiences, that "challenge," as he called it, hardly deserved the title.

In memory of his broken-down motorcycle, his fighter pilot's call sign was "Crazy Horse." Still, at the outset, he thought the Air Force was going to be just an adventure, not a career. "Remember," he said 35 years later, "there was no military tradition in my family. My mother wanted me to be a dentist. My Dad was proud of my going into the military; and he thought it great that I was going to be a flier. My mother thought it was a disaster."

The first adventure he recalls vividly occurred in 1959, while he was an instructor-pilot at a Texas training base. He had just lifted his T-33, two-seat trainer off the runway, and sucked up its landing gear, when the plane's engine blew apart. Immediately, he popped the fuel tanks off his wing tips; pulled up, sacrificing speed to gain altitude; then reacted as many pilots do at the start of a crisis. "I felt I had all kinds of time; as if I was driving a car on a sheet of ice, going nowhere, trying to get traction."

Fortunately, the T-33 was not burning. The rulebook says the first thing he's supposed to do is eject; or, if he can't for some reason, glide the plane straight ahead to belly-flop in a field. He did neither. During the next two to three minutes, he did a wing-over, declared an emergency, and glided back to base, just missing a head-on collision with a student pilot. "The experience," said Abrahamson, "is what fighter pilots call flying: hours and hours of boredom—and a few minutes of stark terror. That became, really, a theme of my life."

Over the next dozen years, he built a reputation for success in a wide variety of assignments. Among those noted most in his ERs (efficiency reports): a master's degree in aeronautical engineering from the University of Oklahoma; being project officer on a nuclear detection satellite development (a small first step toward SDI); flying 49 missions and earning five combat decorations in Vietnam from 1964 to 1965; and being the "salutatorian" graduate of the Air Force Test Pilots School in 1967.

He then joined the Air Force's $100 million Manned Orbiting Laboratory (MOL) program. There, he wrote the first government contract that paid performance bonuses directly to, in this case, flight-simulator operations and maintenance crews rather than to the companies they worked for. He also trained as an MOL astronaut. That ambition evaporated, however, when the program was canceled in 1969, halting plans to put a military/scientific space station into permanent, near-Earth orbit. (The Soviet version has been in orbit for more than a decade now.)

From that instant obscurity, Abrahamson jumped to high-level notice in 1971 when he was named Maverick program director. Under Abrahamson, it was one of the first projects to buy research, development and production, all under one contract, for a system never before invented. And, it was the only one where use of that contracting strategy did not result in excessive cost, or flawed equipment, or both. Abrahamson also learned, on Maverick, that "my boss [General George Brown, then-commander of the Air Force Systems Command] was a teacher of the first order."

The lesson Brown taught involved Abrahamson wanting to flight-test Maverick under its likely operational conditions in Europe. Until then, it had been tested only in the desert on a clear day. In Europe, by contrast, it's raining, foggy, or overcast about 80% of the time. Lieutenant Colonel Abrahamson asked a brigadier general in TAC (Tactical Air Command), the com-

Lieutenant General James A. Abrahamson

mand responsible for all Air Force combat-operational fighter aircraft, to loan him some aircraft and crews to run the tests.

The general turned him down, bluntly noting, "TAC, not [Air Force] Systems Command, is supposed to do operational testing," and "TAC does not do tests in USAFE [U.S. Air Forces Europe] territory." Abe went home and appealed to Brown, saying, "That doesn't make sense." Brown not only agreed, but also got the secretary of the Air Force to do the same. In a subsequent call to his brigadier general adversary at TAC headquarters, Abrahamson reported, "We're going to do an 'Engineering Test' of Maverick in Europe; but when we do it, you'll have a hard time finding any difference between our 'Engineering Test' and the 'Operational' tests you do."

"The little general was livid," said Abrahamson, "but Brown had taught me: 'Do what's right.' He'd also taught me one of the ways to do it." Abrahamson would be put under the spotlight again as program-director in 1976; and would remain a focus of national, even international, attention, until he retired in 1989.

First, he was director of development, test, and initial production of the highly complex (and deadly) F-16 fighter aircraft. A multinational program, it involved four U.S. partners in Europe; five assembly lines; thousands of component parts crisscrossing the Atlantic; even Abe running a bank to manage the partnership currency exchange. Said he of the program, in 1979, "This is the most fun around." His most valuable contribution to the F-16 may have been pressuring Congress into promising it a stable, multi-year budget. From that base, he wrote multi-year contracts with major contractors. Those cut estimated program costs by $500 million. But, more importantly, they inspired contractors to invest their own capital and best people in the program.

Between 1981 and 1984, Abrahamson worked at NASA (National Aeronautics and Space Administration) as associate administrator for space shuttle operations, where he started a worldwide marketing program, promoting shuttle use. By 1983, annual sales were over $1 billion. High school students, however, had more regard for the long-dormant NASA Secondary School Program he fired up. (In 1983 alone, they proposed 8,000 experiments to be done on the shuttle.) He became known publicly as "Abe Abrahamson: Shuttle Super Salesman."

Military Leaders Since World War II

Abrahamson about to brief former Secretary of State Henry Kissinger on "Star Wars."
(Department of Defense photo)

He was firmly convinced, he said at the time, that, "The United States will establish a permanent presence in Space . . . building great enterprises to benefit large numbers of people." To that end, he started a program to make shuttle operations as safely manageable as a commercial airline's. His goal was to position shuttle operations so they could run easily under any one of several arrangements: government only; a semi-public corporation as the Post Office is; or a private company under federal regulation.

These innovative ideas about space shuttle management became academic after the tragic accident of the shuttle *Challenger* in January, 1986, due to a breakdown of the O-rings in its launch boosters. (On Abrahamson's list of things to do, still undone two years after he left NASA, was an investigation of "possible difficulty with booster O-rings.") One price of that failure has been a sharp cutback in funding, so deep that all of NASA is now hobbled. By then, however, Abrahamson had

Lieutenant General James A. Abrahamson

acquired a new set of problems, being named director of the Strategic Defense Initiative (SDI) program in April 1984.

SDI was launched by President Ronald Reagan in March 1983, when he announced, "I would rather defend the American people than avenge them." Abrahamson was hired to head it a year later, after only one interview with Secretary of Defense Caspar Weinberger. What convinced Weinberger to make the appointment was, he said, that "Abe was an expert advocate" of SDI's objective, its merits, and the probability of its engineering success. "His briefings were sufficiently impressive," Weinberger added, "that both British Prime Minister Margaret Thatcher and Prime Minister Rajiv Gandhi of India asked for a repeat performance."

The evolution of Abrahamson's own opinion about SDI, during his tenure, is, itself, interesting. Initially, Abe faced three basic SDI questions: (1) Can we do it technologically?; (2) Can the massive computer-driven computations it will require be developed so the military can control it?; and, finally, (3) Will Congress, and the American people, be willing to support it? By the end of 1985, he said, "There is absolutely no doubt we can make a system that works technically and is survivable." By the end of 1987, he was saying the same thing about SDI's command-and-control system.

Thus, when he retired in 1989 from both the SDI program and the Air Force, only one unanswered SDI question remained as far as he was concerned: "Will Congress, and the American people, support it?" As he told a congressional committee that year, "In 1984, we started with an estimate that SDI would cost $250 billion to develop and deploy. Now, [in 1989] the estimated cost is down to $55 billion." Given that, Weinberger, at least, thought it "petty and unwarranted abuse of a skilled and deserving officer" that the Senate refused to approve Abe's promotion to four-star general "simply because he was leader of the SDI program."

Abrahamson knows well, as dozens of leaders have noted throughout military history, that program success—whether in battles like the Persian Gulf War or in the creation of "Star Wars" type systems—usually requires two things. One is an enormous amount of teamwork. The other is attention to detail. The successful leader inspires the first and stays constantly informed about the details.

Abrahamson also knows both the space shuttle and SDI are that kind of demanding program. Is it merely coincidence that both began to suffer terrible pain, missed deadlines, drastic budget cuts, key personnel turnover and equipment breakdowns—all after he no longer was their team captain?

Chronology

May 19, 1933	James Alan Abrahamson born in Williston, North Dakota
1955	graduates from Massachusetts Institute of Technology with a bachelor's degree in aeronautical engineering and an Air Force second lieutenant's commission
1958	having completed flight training, graduates from Squadron Officer School
1961	earns master's degree in aeronautical engineering from Oklahoma University and becomes project officer on the VELA Nuclear-Detection Satellite Program
1964	assigned for a year to fly fighter missions in Vietnam
1967	after graduation from Test Pilot School, is assigned to the Air Force Manned Orbiting Laboratory program as an engineer and astronaut until program cancellation in 1969
1971	named director of the Maverick air-to-ground missile development program
1976	named director of development and production for the F-16 fighter aircraft program
1981–1984	assigned to the National Aeronautics and Space Administration (NASA) as

Lieutenant General James A. Abrahamson

associate director for manned space flight (director of the Space Shuttle program)

1984–1989 serves as director of the military Strategic Defense Initiative research and development program until he resigns on February 1, 1989. Abrahamson now is executive vice president for corporate development for the Hughes Aircraft Company, a division of General Motors

Decorations: his medals and awards include 3DSM (one from NASA), 2DDSM, 2LM, 2AM, Department of Energy Exceptional Public Service Award, the Goddard Space Flight Trophy, Society of Mechanical Engineers' Outstanding Engineer award, American Astronautical Society's Military Astronautics award, two Daedalian Program Management awards and the Air Force Association's Ira C. Eaker award, to name a few.

Further Reading

"F-16: Spearhead for a Lot of Procurement Innovation?" *Government Executive*, October 1979, pp. 20–21.

Gilmartin, Trish. "Abrahamson Foresees Eventual Drop in SDI Costs," *Defense News*, March 28, 1988, p. 11.

Mohr, Henry. "Improving the Odds for SDI?" *The Washington Times*, March 21, 1989, p. F-4

Sharpless, Jack. "Lt. Gen. James A. Abrahamson," in *The Earthbound Observer*. Michigan City: The Sharpless Corporation, 1983.

"Space Defense: Doable and Affordable," *Government Executive*, September 1984, p. 10.

"The Space Shuttle's Abrahamson: It's Potential is Immense," *Government Executive*, July/August 1983, pp. 11–14.

"Star Warriors: The People Behind the Weapons of the Future," *Newsweek*, June 17, 1985.

"Star Wars," *Time*, March 11, 1985.

"Star Wars Games: The Stakes Go Up," *Time*, June 23, 1986.

Weinberger, Caspar. *Fighting for Peace: Seven Critical Years in the Pentagon*. New York: Warner Books, 1990, pp. 311–317.

"Why the Critics' Attitude is Obsolete," *Government Executive*, January, 1987, p. 12.

INDEX
Bold numbers indicate main headings

A

"Abe's Brigade," 47, 48–49
ABM (anti-ballistic missile): and Patriot, x, 74, 113–114. *See also* SDI (Strategic Defense Initiative)
Abrahamson, Lt. General James A., **113–124**
Abrams, General Creighton W., x, **34–44**, 50, 72, 103–104, 110
Adler, Larry, 46
Airborne Infantry: and Abrams/Brown, 103–105; and Powell, 6–8; and Ridgway, 14; and Rowny, 46, 50; and Westmoreland, 27. *See also* AirLand Battle Doctrine
Air Force: 18, 26,49–50, 61, 64, 72, 107–108; and Air Force Systems Command, 104, 114n, 118–119; and "Air Power," 18, 49, 61, 71, 85, 102; and Commander, Air Operations, MACV, 103–104; and North American Air Defense Command, 109; and Tactical Air Command (TAC), 104, 118–119
Air Force Chief of Staff: x, 36, 104, 107, 108–109.
AirLand Battle Doctrine, xi–xii, 7 (implied), 27, 49–50, 101–105
Almond, Major General Edward M., 48 (photograph)
American University, 45
Annapolis, 24, 57, 58, 69–70, 75, 80–81
"Anti-militarism," 74
Anti–submarine Warfare (ASW), 72, 86–87, 109
Arizona (battleship), 58
Armed Forces Special Weapons Project, 84
Army Air Corps. *See* Air Force
Army Chief of Staff: x, 13, 18, 26n, 27–28, 31, 39, 41–42, 49, 104, 112; and Vice Chief of Staff, 35
Army Command and General Staff College, 4, 13, 32
Army General Staff: and Army War Plans Division of, 13; and the Deputy Chief of Staff, Administration, of, 14; and the G-3 (Operations) office of, 41; and the Operations and Planning Division (OPD) of, 27, 48–49; and the Secretary of, 28; and the Strategy, Plans, and Policy Office of, 5; and the Army Doctrine Command, 104
Army War College, 13, 27
Atomic Energy Commission, 84, 85
AWACS (Airborne Warning and Control System), 109

B

B-1 Bomber (and B-70 bomber), 108, 109
Berlin, Germany 47
Bjorkgren, Anders, 57
Bolivia, 13
Boy Scouts of America, 23, 105
Bradley, General Omar, 12n,
Brady, Father John J., 81
Brazil, 13
Brown, General George S., x, 51, 72, 74, **101–112**, 118–119
Brown, Mrs. Alice "Skip," 106. *See also* "Acknowledgments"
Brown University, 40
Burke, Admiral Arleigh A., x, **56–66**, 67, 71, 84, 86
Burke, August, 57
Burke, Oscar and Clara Mokler Burke (Arleigh Burke's parents), 57
Bush, President George, 7, 101
Byrnes, Secretary of State James F., 24

C

California Institute of Technology (CalTech), 84, 85, 115
Cambodia, 30, 36
Carlucci, Defense Secretary Frank, 5–6
Carter, President Jimmy, 109
CBS-TV News, 22–23
Center for Strategic and International Studies, 57
CFRE (Conventional Forces Reduction, Europe), treaty, 52–53
Challenger (space shuttle), 120
Chicago Bears, 91
Chief of Naval Operations (CNO): 56, 61, 63–64, 67, 71–74; and Deputy

Index

CNO for Research and Development, 86; and OP-23 (Assistant CNO for Organizational Research and Policy), 61; and OP-30 (Director of Strategic Plans), 63
China Lake, and Naval Weapons Center, 84–86
Chinese Communist army, 15–17, 36, 63–64, 94
Citadel, The, 24
City College of New York, 2
Civil Rights movement. *See* Leadership, Military
Clay, General Lucius, 110
Coast Guard, 82
"Cold War," vii–ix
Colorado School of Mines, 91
Colorado State University, 91
Combat Command: and rotation to staff duty (Powell example), 3–4; and Burke's "Little Beavers," 59. *See also* Leadership
Combined Action Platoon (CAP), 95–97. *See also* Vietnam War
Congress' Role in National Security: ix–xi, 15, 46, 62, 72–73, 78–79, 80, 85, 109, 114, 118, 119, 121; and appointments to the Joint Chiefs of Staff, 67, 72; and officer promotions, 69, 97, 130; and Arms-Reduction Treaties, 52; and Vietnam War, 36–37, 42, 72–73
Counter–insurgency warfare, anti-guerrilla operations: 26–27, 30, 94–97; and Army Special Warfare Course, 3; and helicopters, 51–52; and RECONDO (Reconnaissance and Commando) training, 26–27. *See also* Decision-making
Cuban Missile Crisis, 86

D

Davis, General Benjamin O. and Benjamin, O., Jr., 1n
Davis, Major General R. G., 92
Dawkins, Brig. General Peter, 5
Decision–making: in combat command, "decide quickly and on your own," 11–12, 14, 27–28, 59–60, 95–97, 109–110; on major policies and programs, x–xi, 28, 49–50; nature and kinds of, 45–46, 97–98, 129–130; as a program director, 85–86, 104, 114; and salesmanship, 83–87, 109, 121; and teamwork, 104, 114, 121. *See also* Leadership, Military

Dixon, General Robert J., 103, 109
Duke University, 110

E

Easter-tide Offensive, 73. *See also* Vietnam War
Education: and career success, 4–5, 46–47, 64, 68, 105–106; and failure, 69, 115–116; as a family responsibility, 68, 115–117; and the importance of schoolwork concentration, 2–3, 12, 40, 57–58, 69–70, 79–81, 82–84, 115; and objections to discipline, 68, 79–81; in a one-room schoolhouse, 57, 64; of an orphan, 91–92. *See also* Teachers' influence
Egypt, 73–74, 109
Eisenhower, President Dwight D., 14, 17, 18–19, 63
Enterprise (aircraft carrier), 86
Eufaula, Alabama, 68

F

F–16 fighter aircraft, 119
Foreign Policy: 13, 14–15, 16–18, 26n, 28–29, 46, 48–49, 71–75, 82, 92–93, 95, 108; and military planning, 18–19, 71n, 72–73, 95–97; and terrorists, limited-war confrontation, 93, 95–97, 101–103. *See also* Treaties
Forrestal, Defense Secretary James V., vii–ix, 85

G

Gandhi, Indian Prime Minister Rajiv, 121
Gates, Defense Secretary Thomas S., Jr., xi, 107, 108
Gavin, General James M., 27
Georgia Tech University, 68
George II, British King, 23
George Washington University, 5
Gerrard-Gough, Dr., J. D., and "Chick" Hayward, 86
Giap, Vo Nguyen. *See* Vo Nguyen Giap
Golan Heights, 74
Goodpaster, General Andrew, 17, 23, 40–41, 53
Graham, Lt. General Daniel O., 23
Grant, General Ulysses S., 40
"Great Depression," 68–69, 82, 91
Gulf of Tonkin Resolution, 4, 35, 71n

126

Index

H

Haiphong Harbor, North Vietnam, 36, 71n, 73 *See also* Vietnam War
Halsey, Admiral William F. "Bull," 59–60
Hayward, Charles Brian, 79
Hayward, Vice Admiral John T., 72, **78–89**
Hazelhurst Flying Field, 79
Helicopters: 96; and Air Medical Evacuation, 50–51; and " Swarm of Bees" combat tactic, 50. *See also* Airborne Infantry
Ho Chi Minh Trail, 36. *See also* Vietnam War
Hodes, Major General Henry, 63
Honduras, 82
Hussein, Iraqi dictator Saddam, 101–102, 114

I

Indochina (Laos, Cambodia, Vietnam), 18–19, 30
Indonesia, 70
Infantry Schools, 3, 11, 13, 48, 50
Iraq, x, 7, 101–103, 113–114
Israel: 102; and Yom Kippur and Six Days War, 74, 109–110

J

Jackson, Senator Henry M. "Scoop," 51
James, General Daniel "Chappie," Jr., 1n, 5
Japanese: 15, 59, 70, 84, 93; and their Self-Defense Force, 48; and Japanese World War II strategy, 70–71
Johns Hopkins University, 47–48
Johnson, Alma Vivian (wife of General Colin Powell), 3
Johnson, President Lyndon B., 29, 35, 72
Johnson, Secretary of Defense Louis A., 61
Joint Chiefs of Staff: 15, 49–52; and as advisors to civilian leadership, viii–xi, 15–17, 28, 49, 72–74; and Army-Navy-Air Force competition, 61–62; and the Chairman of the, 1, 6–8, 12n, 26n, 38, 51–52, 67, 104, 107, 109–110
Joint Strategic Planning Group, 107
Joy, Admiral C. Turner, and Korean truce talks, 62–63

K

Kennedy, Robert F. "Bobby," 42
Kennedy, President John F., 26n, 29, 41–42
Korean War, 14–17, 27, 29, 37, 46, 48, 50, 93, 107, 116; and Air Medical Evacuation, 50–51; and Korean Airlift, 107; and United Nations Military Armistice negotiations team, 62; and wasted sacrifice of lives, 94. *See also* Treaties
Kosciusko, Polish General Thaddeus, 47n

L

Laird, Defense Secretary Melvin R., 37
Laos, 30, 36
Leadership, Military: 25–26, 27–28; and anticipating the future, xi, 15–16, 49 ("dream sessions"), 59–60, 61, 63, 72–75, 86, 93– 94, 121; and Army-Navy-Air Force competition, 64, 85, 107–108; and civil rights movement, 1–5, 17n, 41–42; and training for, 26– 27, 40–41, 63–64, 74, 83–85, 87, 91; and ego, 58–59; and five rules for exercise of, 85–86; and integrity, 23–26, 41, 52–53, 58–59, 86, 96–97, 107–108, 110; and opposition to war, 6, 15, 97; and salesmanship, 85, 114, 121; and talents needed for, ix–xi, 91–92, 104, 107, 119
Lee, General Robert E., 40
LeMay, General Curtis, on bombing in Vietnam War, 36
Lewis, Kirk, 52
Lincoln, General George "Abe," 47–49
"Little Beavers," 59, 84

M

M1A1 "Abrams" tank, 41n
MacArthur, General Douglas, 13, 15–16, 47
McDonald, Admiral David L., 72
McNamara, Defense Secretary Robert S.: and "cost-effective analysis," 35–36, 95; and Brown, 108–109; and Vietnam War, 30
MACV (U.S. Military Assistance Command, Vietnam). *See* Vietnam War
Management and Budget, Office of, 5

Index

Marine Corps Assistant Commandant, 97
Marine Corps Schools, 93, 94
Marshall, General George C., vii, ix, 11–13, 17
Massachusetts Institute of Technology (MIT), 115–116
Maverick air-to-ground, "smart," guided bomb, 113, 118–119
MBFR (Mutual Balanced Force Reduction) in Europe, planning and negotiations for, 51–53. *See also* CFRE
Medals, key to, xi–xiv
Meese, Attorney General Edwin, 2
Military Academy, U.S. *See* West Point
Military Assistant to the Secretary of Defense; and to the President: 1, 107; and importance of, 5–8, 36, 41–42, 107–109; and similarity to Secretary of the Army General Staff, 28.
Military Leadership. *See* Leadership, Military
Miller, Rear Admiral Henry L., 63
MIT. *See* Massachusetts Institute of Technology
Mitscher, Admiral Marc A. "Pete," 60–61, 86
Moorer, Richard Randolph, 68
Moorer, Admiral Thomas H., 56, **67–77**, 110
Morale, *esprit de corps:* and Code of Ethics, 23, 25–26, 97–98; and importance of, ix, 4, 36, 121; and Korean War, "We're going North," 15–17; and "making heroes," x; and Vietnam War, 36, 39, 42
Mugford, (destroyer), 59

N

NASA (National Aeronautics and Space Administration), 119
National Football League, 92n
National Guard: 35, 47, 105; and Air National Guard, 109
National Security Council, and National Security Advisor, 5–6
National Security: and "cost-effective" analysis of, 35–36; and economic and diplomatic aspects of, vii–x, 72–74, 94 (Korean "traitors"), 97; and the importance of naval forces, 58, 61, 71; and problems of being prepared for war, vii–x, 17–18, 74, 84, 121–122; and "Revolt of the Admirals," 61–62, 85; and spending for, 17–18, 42, 47, 72–75, 78–79, 104, 109, 114, 119–122;

and strategy of "flexible response," 27–29, 46, 49, 71, 95; and technology aspects of, viii–x, 56, 84–85, 113–114, 118–121. *See also* Foreign Policy
NATO (North Atlantic Treaty Organization): viii, 14–15, 17, 49; and SHAPE/SACEUR (Supreme Headquarters, Allied Powers in Europe/Supreme Allied Commander, Europe), 17–18, 45–46, 49, 51; and Air-Land Battle Doctrine, 102.
National War College, 5, 57, 107
Naval Academy, U.S. *See* Annapolis
Naval Gun Factory, 63
Naval Ordnance Test Station, Inyokern, Calif. *See* China Lake
Naval War College, 57, 78, 87
Navy General Board, 61
New York University, 2
New York Yankees, 79–80
Nicaragua, 13
Nixon, President Richard M., 37, 73
Nobel Peace Prize, vii (footnote)
Noriega, Panamanian dictator Manuel, 6–7
Norstad, General Lauris, 49
Norton, Lt. General John "Jack," 14, 35, 36, 47, 105–106

O

Oakdale Military Academy, 79
O'Meara, General Andrew P., 51
Organization of American States (OAS) and Inter-American Defense Board, 14

P

Palmer, General Bruce, Jr., 38–40, 42–43
Panama Canal, and dictator Manuel Noriega, 6–7
Paraguay, 13
Parental influence: on Abrahamson, 114–117; on Abrams, 34, 40; on Brown, 105–106; on Burke, 57–58; on Hayward, 79–82; on Moorer, 68–69; on Powell, 2, 4, 8; on Ridgway, 12; on Rowny, 46; on Westmoreland, 23–24
Patriot anti-missile missile, x, 113–114
Patton, General George S., Jr., on Abrams, 41
Pearl Harbor, 58n, 59, 70–71, 84
Pershing, General John J. "Blackjack," 25–26
Pershing Rifles, 2

128

Index

Persian Gulf War, x, 7–8, 35, 41n, 101–105, 109, 113–114, 121
Philippine Islands, 13, 715
Pilot-Training Schools: rigors of, 75, 87–89, 126–127
Porter, General Robert, 47
Powell, General Colin, **1–10,** 102
Powell, Luther, 2
Puller, General Lewis B., "Chesty," A "Marine's Marine," 91, 930

R

Reagan, President Ronald, 2, 5–6, 74, 121
"Revolt of the Admirals," 61
Rickover, Rear Admiral Hyman, 63
Ridgway, General Matthew B., **11–21,** 26–27, 28, 36, 62–63
Ridgway, Thomas, 12
Rogers, Lt. Colonel James D., 97
Roosevelt, President Franklin D., 1n, 71
ROTC (Reserve Officers Training Corps), 2, 47, 91, 117
Rowan, columnist Carl, 2, 4
Rowny, Lt. General Edward L., 14, 15–16, **45–55,** 105. *See also* "Acknowledgments"
Rusk, Secretary of State Dean, 29, 48

S

SACEUR (Supreme Allied Commander, Europe), 17–18, 49. *See also* NATO
Schwar, Joseph, 8
Schwarzkopf, General H. Norman, 102
Scratchley, H. P., 106
Scud missile, x, 102. 113–114
SDI (Strategic Defense Initiative): 74, 114, 120–122; and the Manned Orbiting Laboratory (MOL), 118. *See also* ABM
Senate Armed Services Committee, 72
Senate Foreign Affairs Committee, 52
Sergeant anti-ballistic missile, x
SHAPE (Supreme Headquarters, Allied Powers Europe), 17, 45. *See also* NATO
Sherman, Admiral Forrest, 61–62
Skantze, General Lawrence A., 104, 114n
Smith, Lt. General DeWitt C., Jr., 41
Solomon Islands, 60, 93
Soviet Union: viii, 36, 49, 61; and arms-reduction treaties, 46, 51–53, 74; and difficulty of defeating in war, 18; and KGB agents, 17; and Korean War, 15–16, 62–63; and the Middle East, 74, 113; and Soviet SDI, 74, 118; and Vietnam War, 36, 71n, 95; and worldwide Soviet Navy deployment, 72
Space Shuttle: 49; and its possible future, 119–120
Sprint anti-ballistic missile, x
Stanford University, 84
"Star Wars." *See* SDI
SALT (Strategic Arms Limitation Treaties), 46, 51, 74. *See also* Treaties
Steinhoff, German General Johannes, 51
Strategic Bombing Survey/Japan, 70–71
"Swarm of Bees," The, 50
Sykes, Captain James B., 85–86
Syria, 73, 109

T

Taylor, General Maxwell D., 26, 26n, 28
Teachers' influence: on Abrahamson, 115–117; on Abrams, 40; on Burke, 57–58; on Hayward, 79–81; on Moorer, 68–69; on Rowny, 44–47; on Walt, 91–92
Temple University, 83
Thatcher, British Prime Minister Margaret, 121
Thayer, Deputy Secretary of Defense Paul W., x
Thurman, General Maxwell, 6
Time magazine, 16
Tomahawk cruise missile, 102
Tower, Senator John, 72
Treaties: and Conventional Forces in Europe (CFE), formerly called Mutual Balanced Force Reductions (MBFR) treaty, 51–53; and Korean War, 17–18, 62–63; and Strategic Arms Limitations Treaty 46, 51–53, 74; and Vietnam War, 42, 73. *See also* Foreign Policy; *See also* National Security
Truman, President Harry S., 15–16, 19, 24, 61, 63

U

UN (United Nations): 14; and Korean truce talks, 62–63
U.S. Military Academy. *See* West Point
U.S. Naval Academy. *See* Annapolis
University of Colorado, 58
University of Michigan, 58

Index

University of Mississippi, 41
University of Missouri, 105
University of New Mexico, 84
University of Oklahoma, 118
University of Pennsylvania, 83

V

Valkyries, Ride of the, 39
Vietnam War: 4, 8, 28–29, 34, 71n, 94–97, 108–109; and Army Concept Team, 50; and MACV, 4, 22, 26n, 28–31, 36, 73, 103–104; and military victories, 40, 73, 95–96; and "Peace" Treaty, 42, 73; and Press coverage, 22–23 (Westmoreland), 28–29, 38, 95–96; and Ridgway opposition to, 18; and Tet offensive, 23, 30; and training South Vietnamese, 37–38, 72–73, 95–96; and war-fighting strategies, 36–37, 42, 71n, 94–97; and withdrawal from, 37–38, 73
Virginia Military Institute, 24
Vo Nguyen Giap, North Vietnamese General, 31, 40

W

Walker, General Walton H. and Korea, 15
Wallace, Alabama Governor George, 41
Walt, General Lewis W., 90–100
Washington Post, The, 5, 8

Washington, President George, ix
Watergate scandal, 42
Watson, Colonel Sam, 51
WeinWeinberger, Defense Secretary Caspar, 4–5, 121
Westmoreland, General William C., **22–33,** 37, 38–41
West Point: 12–13, 24–25, 27, 40–41, 47, 51, 58, 69, 105–106; and First Captain of Cadets, 24, 105; and U.S. Military Academy Superintendent, 13 (MacArthur), 27 (Westmoreland)
Wheeler, General Earle W., 108–109
White, General Thomas D., 107
White House, ix, 1, 6, 40–41, 61, 74, 85; and the "eager beavers," 38; and a White House Fellow, 5
Wilson, Defense Secretary Charles E., 18
Wright Brothers, Orville and Wilbur, 79
World War II: vii, 45, 49; and Abrams, 34, 41; and Brown, 106–107; and Burke, 59–60; and Hayward, 83–84; and Moorer, 70–71; and Ridgway, 13–14; and Rowny, 47–49; and Walt, 93; and Westmoreland, 26–27

Y

Yale University, 50
Yamamoto, Japanese Admiral Isoroku, 71
Yom Kippur War, 73–74, 109–110